C000061430

Classics

SOMERSET
COUNTY CRICKET CLUB

Taunton Cricket Ground, around 1900.

Taunton Cricket Ground, around 1990.

Classics

SOMERSET

COUNTY CRICKET CLUB

EDDIE LAWRENCE

TEMPUS

First published 2002
Copyright © Eddie Lawrence, 2002

Tempus Publishing Limited
The Mill, Brimscombe Port,
Stroud, Gloucestershire, GL5 2QG

ISBN 0 7524 2409 2

Typesetting and origination by
Tempus Publishing Limited
Printed in Great Britain by
Midway Colour Print, Wiltshire

INTRODUCTION

To the end of the 2001 cricket season, Somerset had played over 2,400 first-class matches and more than 700 one-day games.

After much debate, it was decided to restrict this selection to first-class matches only. It might well be that a second book dealing only with one-day games will be published at some future date.

How should one select these fifty matches? Outstanding individual performances, outstanding victories and losses, exciting finishes and curious happenings were all taken into account; an attempt was also made to spread the collection over the 109 years of first-class cricket.

Many of the matches took place in the dim and distant past and contemporary accounts have been the author's main source of information; those games played between the 1930s and 1960s were enriched by talking to some of the surviving players and many of the later games were actually witnessed at first hand.

Somerset yearbooks, *Wisdens*, *The Cricketer* and books written by Ron Roberts, Peter Roebuck, David Foot and Vic Marks have been of tremendous help and whilst it is not expected that everyone will agree with the final selection, it is hoped that pleasant memories will be revived.

Finally, I am very grateful to Mike Tarr for permission to reproduce many of his superb portraits of leading players.

Is this the future?

SOMERSET OFFICIALS 1891-2001

Year	President	Year	Secretary
1891-1915	Hon. Sir Spencer Ponsonby-Fane, B.T.	1913-1919	R. Brooks-King
		1920-1922	S.M.J. Woods
1916-1922	H.E. Murray Anderdon	1923-1931	A.F. Davey
1923	A.E. Newton	1932-1936	J. Daniell
1924	The Marquis of Bath, K.G.	1937-1949	Brig. E.H. Lancaster
1925	Lt-Col. Sir Dennis F. Boles, B.T.	1950	N.J.C. Daniell
1926	Col. H.M. Ridley	1950-1955	Air Vice-Marshall M.L. Taylor
1927	Rev. Preb. A.P. Wickham	1955-1969	R. Robinson
1928	Col. H.M. Ridley	1970-1975	A.K. James
1929	L.C.H. Palairet	1975-1979	R.G. Stevens
1930	V.T. Hill	1979-1982	D.G. Seward
1931-1932	Major A.G. Barrett	1982-1988	A.S. Brown
1933	Lt-Col. W.O. Gibbs	1988	P.W. Anderson

Year	Chairman
	Until 1952 the President of the club also acted as Chairman

Year	President	Year	Chairman
1934-1935	Lt-Col. Sir Dennis Boles, B.T.		
1936	The Duke of Somerset	1952-1953	Major G.E. Longrigg
1937-1946	R.C.N. Palairet	1954-1959	A.H. Southwood
1946-1949	J. Daniell	1960-1969	E.F. Longrigg
1950-1953	Major G.E. Longrigg	1969-1971	Lt-Col. G.C.G. Grey
1954-1960	The Bishop of Bath & Wells	1972-1973	C.R.M. Atkinson
1961	J.C. White	1974-1976	H.W. Hoskins
1962-1965	W.T. Greswell	1977-1978	L.G. Creed
1966-1967	Lord Hylton	1979	R.C. Kerslake
1968-1971	E.F. Longrigg	1979-1982	J.M. Jeffrey
1971-1976	R.V. Showering	1983-1987	M.F. Hill
1976-1991	C.R.M. Atkinson	1987-1988	A.J. Gardner
1991-1996	J. Luff	1988-	R. Parsons
1996-	M.F. Hill		

SOMERSET CAPTAINS 1882-2000

Year	Captain	Year	Captain
1882-1884	S.C. Newton	1953-1954	B.G. Brocklehurst
1885	E. Sainsbury	1955	G.G. Tordoff
1891-1893	H.T. Hewett	1956-1959	M.F. Tremlett
1894-1906	S.M.J. Woods	1960-1964	H.W. Stephenson
1907	L.C.H. Palairet	1965-1967	C.R.M. Atkinson
1908-1912	J. Daniell	1968	R.C. Kerslake
1913-1914	E.S.M. Poyntz	1969-1971	B.A. Langford
1919-1926	J. Daniell	1972-1977	D.B. Close
1927-1931	J.C. White	1978-1983	B.C. Rose
1932-1937	R.A. Ingle	1984-1985	I.T. Botham
1938-1946	E.F. Longrigg	1986-1988	P.M. Roebuck
1947	R.J.O. Meyer	Aug 88-89	V.J. Marks
1948	N.S. Mitchell-Innes	1990-1993	C.J. Tavare
	G.E.S. Woodhouse	1994-1996	A.N. Hayhurst
	J.W. Seamer	1997-1998	P.D. Bowler
1949	G.E.S. Woodhouse	1999-	J. Cox
1950-1952	S.S. Rogers		

FOREWORD

Following the success of his recent book, *Somerset CCC Greats*, Eddie Lawrence has turned his attention to selecting fifty of Somerset's most memorable matches.

Since Somerset have played nearly 2,500 first-class fixtures, all but a couple of hundred or so in the County Championship, he has set himself a challenging task. It has been accomplished through the unquenchable enthusiasm of one who, although Yorkshire born and subsequently spending twenty-five years in Kent, has developed a love and deep knowledge of Somerset cricket since making the county his home.

The matches chosen cover the period from the time when Somerset were admitted to the County Championship in 1891, although there were many exciting games prior to this date. For the early decades the author has had to rely solely on contemporary accounts, such as when Archie MacLaren scored over half of Lancashire's total of 801 at Taunton in 1895. To this era also belong matches from which lowly Somerset gained the reputation of being 'the team of surprises'. The amazing victory over mighty Yorkshire in 1901 when all seemed lost must surely rank as one of the most remarkable in the history of the entire Championship. But Somerset's memorable matches also include many within living memory. Think of Somerset *v*. Lancashire at Taunton in 1993, for example, when the visitors, needing only 88 for victory and with plenty of time in hand, met defeat with Andy Caddick taking 9 for 32.

Some of the most unforgettable occasions have been when the result has depended on what was literally the last delivery. In the inter-war years Somerset had no fewer than three tied matches. That game against Sussex at Taunton in 1919 had one of the strangest endings to any cricket match anywhere in the world.

One or two matches other than those in the County Championship have earned their place in the book. There are still many of the older generation of supporters who will treasure memories of the visit of the Indians in 1946, when record crowds sat in the sun and saw the visitors decisively defeated. There was also that glorious victory over the Australians at Bath just over thirty years later.

Eddie Lawrence has been watching cricket since his boyhood in the 1930s, and has seen it played all around the world. In his years in Somerset he has done much for the County Club, as well as nationally for the Lord's Taverners and once again he is dividing his royalties between the Taverners and our museum.

He has provided another welcome treat for all who, like him, love Somerset cricket.

Tony Stedall
Curator

FOUR SOMERSET CAPTAINS.

H.W. Hewett.

M. Tremlett.

D.B. Close.

B.C. Rose.

THE 50 CLASSIC MATCHES

1891	v. Kent	at Maidstone
1892	v. Yorkshire	at Taunton
1895	v. Lancashire	at Taunton
1895	v. Surrey	at Taunton
1901	v. Yorkshire	at Leeds
1902	v. Yorkshire	at Sheffield
1905	v. The Australians	at Bath
1907	v. Gloucestershire	at Bristol
1907	v. Middlesex	at Lord's
1908	v. Hampshire	at Southampton
1913	v. Worcestershire	at Worcester
1914	v. Gloucestershire	at Bristol
1914	v. Yorkshire	at Weston-Super-Mare
1919	v. Sussex	at Taunton
1920	v. Gloucestershire	at Bristol
1921	v. Worcestershire	at Worcester
1921	v. Gloucestershire	at Bristol
1925	v. Surrey	at Taunton
1926	v. Essex	at Chelmsford
1929	v. Essex	at Chelmsford
1931	v. Surrey	at The Oval
1931	v. Gloucestershire	at Bristol
1933	v. Kent	at Tunbridge Wells
1934	v. Gloucestershire	at Bristol
1935	v. Essex	at Frome
1937	v. Surrey	at The Oval
1938	v. Kent	at Wells
1938	v. Gloucestershire	at Taunton
1938	v. Worcestershire	at Worcester
1939	v. Kent	at Bath
1939	v. Worcestershire	at Kidderminster
1946	v. Glamorgan	at Pontypridd
1946	v. The Indians	at Taunton
1947	v. Middlesex	at Lord's
1947	v. Gloucestershire	at Bristol
1948	v. Sussex	at Eastbourne
1953	v. Lancashire	at Bath
1960	v. Lancashire	at Taunton
1960	v. Cambridge University	at Taunton
1961	v. Surrey	at Taunton
1968	v. The Australians	at Taunton
1976	v. Gloucestershire	at Taunton
1977	v. The Australians	at Bath
1980	v. Gloucestershire	at Bristol
1981	v. Gloucestershire	at Bath
1985	v. Warwickshire	at Taunton
1988	v. Worcestershire	at Taunton
1991	v. Lancashire	at Taunton
1991	v. Warwickshire	at Taunton
1993	v. Lancashire	at Taunton

KENT

13, 14 July 1891 at Maidstone

Somerset's first ever County Championship victory was against Kent at that delightful ground, the Mote, Maidstone. It was the first meeting between the two teams and opinions had already been expressed that Somerset were not yet good enough to be a first-class county side.

At the time, Kent were leading the Championship and were undefeated; on winning the toss, they had no hesitation in electing to bat. The fast bowling of Woods unsettled them after an opening stand of 40 and the remaining 9 wickets fell for the addition of only 66. Woods had a great day and finished with 5 wickets for 44, but he received wonderful support from Nicholls who bowled 26 overs, of which 17 were maidens, taking 3 for 15.

After disappointing in earlier games, L.C.H. Palairet and Hewett succeeded in putting together a fine opening partnership, with Palairet scoring an elegant 79, while the boisterous Hewett had to be satisfied with a quick 27. Of the later batsmen, only Challen showed confidence against the good bowling by Martin and with the unnecessary run-out of Nicholls, the innings collapsed to 218 all out – a lead of 112.

With a short time to bat before lunch, Kent lost 2 wickets for only 33 but then fought back well – although all the bowlers made them fight for their runs, with Tyler taking 5 for 45. No batsman reached 50, although there were three scores over 30 in a final total of 160. Wickham had been a great support behind the stumps with 4 stumpings and a catch during two Kent innings. Somerset had only 49 runs to go, and they would have achieved their first victory!

The innings started after tea and there followed 70 minutes of breathtaking cricket before victory was finally assured. Hewett was out for 11 with the score on 13 and L.C.H. Palairet was bowled for 8. With only 28 on the scoreboard, Nicholls was bowled by Wright for 2 and worse was to follow. Woods was bowled by Martin for 1, Tyler failed to score and at 29 for 5 Somerset were in serious trouble. R.C.N. Palairet succeeded where his elder brother had failed and runs again appeared. Helped by Challen, who was lucky not to be caught and extremely lucky to get three runs as a result of the dropped catch, the target was finally reached and so Somerset recorded their first victory.

A.P. Wickham.

SOMERSET v. KENT.

PLAYED AT

MOTE PARK, MAIDSTONE, Monday & Tuesday,

July 13th and 14th, 1891.

Won by 5 Wickets.

KENT.

	First Innings.		Second Innings.	
Mr. L. Wilson	st Wickham, b Nichols	36	st Wickham, b Tyler	13
Hearne, (A.)	st Wickham, b Tyler	22	b Woods	0
Mr. F. Marchant	c Robinson, b Woods	3	b Nichols	39
Mr. C. J. M. Fox	b Nichols	10	b Nichols	36
Mr. H. M. Braybrook	c Hewett, b Nichols	9	c Wickham, b Tyler	40
Mr G. J. V. Weigall	b Woods	4	b Woods	14
Mr. F. de L. Solbe	b Woods	0	st Wickham, b Tyler	1
Hearne, (G.)	run out	4	b Tyler	0
Wright	b Woods	8	b Tyler	6
Martin	not out	4	b Woods	1
Nuttall	b Woods	0	not out	6
	B 4, l-b 2	6	l-b	4
	Total	106	Total	160

SOMERSET.

	First Innings.		Second Innings.	
Mr H. T. Hewett (Capt.)	b A. Hearne	27	b Wright	11
Mr. L. C H. Palairet	c Fox, b Martin	79	b Martin	8
Mr. J. B. Challen	st Nuttall, b Martin	41	not out	18
Mr. C. J. Robinson	b Wright	1		
Mr. G Fowler	b Martin	11		
Nichols	run out	23	b Wright	2
Tyler	l-b w, A. Hearne	13	b Martin	0
Mr. R. C. N. Palairet	c Wilson, b Martin	16	not out	9
Mr. S. M. J. Woods	c Marchant, b G. Hearne	5	b Martin	1
Mr. F. J. Poynton	not out	1		
Rev. A. P. Wickham	b Martin	1		
			l-b	1
	Total	218	Total	50

BOWLING ANALYSIS.

KENT.		1st Innings.				2nd Innings.		
		O.	M.	R.	W.	O.	M.	R.	W.
Mr. Woods		27·3	9	44	5	16	2	65	3
Tyler		21	6	41	1	25	8	45	5
Nichols		26	17	15	3	28	11	46	2

SOMERSET.		1st Innings.				2nd Innings.		
		O.	M.	R.	W.	O.	M.	R.	W.
Martin		43	15	58	5	18	10	19	3
Wright		38	17	57	1	17	7	30	2
Hearne, A.		23	9	51	2	—	—	—	—
Hearne, G.		26	11	31	1	—	—	—	—
Mr. Fox		7	1	21	0	—	—	—	—

Umpires—F. Coward and Tuck.   Scorers—T. H. Knight and J. Crow.

YORKSHIRE

25, 26 August 1892 at Taunton

Having beaten Yorkshire by 87 runs in Sheffield earlier in the season, hopes ran high that the 'double' could be achieved and as each hour passed hopes continued to rise. Yorkshire were without their usual captain, Lord Hawke, and Hunter was captain in his place. On winning the toss, he elected to bat first on a very good wicket; while no batsmen reached a century, consistent run-getting down the order saw them obtain a good 299. Indeed, Smith and Jackson had got them off to a rapid start, scoring 83 runs in 55 minutes. Tyler took 9 wickets at a cost of 111 runs, teasing all the batsmen, and although the side was suffering from the loss of Newton with sore fingers, they found an able deputy in L.C.H. Palairet, who gave a first-class performance in this unusual position.

In the time remaining, Somerset's regular opening pair, L.C.H. Palairet and Hewett, were faced with a somewhat tired Yorkshire attack and Hewett thrashed the first ball of the innings to the boundary and at close of play Somerset were 78 without loss.

The second day was one of runs, runs and more runs, with neither batsmen being troubled by the Yorkshire bowling attack. Hewett was the first to reach 100 – in just two hours – but Palairet soon followed, although he had been dropped at the wicket when his score was 28. The scoring rate reached 100 runs per hour and it was not until 346 runs had been scored that the first wicket fell – a new record for a first-wicket partnership. The first 100 runs only took 65 minutes, the second 100 was even faster, taking just 60 minutes.

When the stand reached 300 – the first time in the history of first-class cricket – the crowd erupted and the lunch interval that followed was one of continuous celebrations. It was not until 3 p.m. that the first wicket fell. Hewett's magnificent innings came to an end when he was bowled by Peel, but not before scoring 201 and also registering his first ever first-class century for Somerset.

Runs continued to flow, Hedley taking over when Palairet finally fell to a sharp slip catch for 146. Hedley went on to score 102 in 150 minutes, another first century for Somerset. A final score of 592 reduced Yorkshire's hopes of saving the game, although Peel bowled 59.3 overs in taking 7 for 133 – a mammoth effort.

The 592 runs were scored in only 173 overs and Yorkshire were faced with scoring 293 to make Somerset bat a second time. With the 'double' over Yorkshire well in sight, Somerset were hoping that their large total would enable them to win on the final day. Unfortunately, cricket's arch-enemy, rain, prevented a ball being bowled, although it was not until the tea interval that play was finally abandoned.

Hewett and Palairet celebrate their 346 first-wicket partnership.

Alphabet on the Somerset XI, 1892

A for the "averages" hard to be beat,
B for the Batsmen so fleet on their feet.
C for the "centuries," Yorkshire's fate sealed,
    Also, for *Challen*, so deft in the field,
D for the "duck's-egg," that's never allowed,
E for the eagerness shewn by the crowd,
F stands for *Fowler*, a good useful hitter,
G is for Gloucester, whose feelings are bitter.
H is for *Hewett* and *Hedley* and *Hill*,
I for the "innings" prolonged by their skill.
K for the "knocks," that poor *Newton* bore,
L for the Leg that is sometimes "before!"
M for the "maidens," our *Sammy*'s just pride,
N is for *Nichols*, who ne'er bowls a "wide."
O for the "overs," that *Woods* makes renown'd,
P is for *Palairet*, a "clinker," all round!
Q for the quartet of bowlers so deadly,
    S.M.J., *Tyler*, *Nichols*, and *Hedley*.
R is for *Robinson*, ne'er caught at wicket,
S is for Somerset, *the* County for Cricket.
T is for *Tyler*, whose "slows," batsmen flurry,
    The terror of Notts. and the envy of Surrey.
U for the Umpire, whose ankle's quite sore,
    With stopping the drive that *Hill* meant for 4.
V for the "'Varsity Blues" in the team
    Of Cricketers verily they are the cream.
W the Wicket-keep, so smart with his catches,
X for the 'xtras, so rare in our matches.
Y for the Yorker, each bowler's ambition,
Z for the zeal which sent Notts. to perdition.

The exploits of Somerset CCC in verse.

A Yorkshire CCC XI in the 1890s. The players are, from left to right, back row: Wardall, Whitehead, Mr Dodworth, Mounsey. Middle row: Tunnicliffe, Peel, Lord Hawke, F.S. Jackson, Wainwright. Front row: Brown, Hunter, Hirst.

Somerset County XI, 1892. From left to right, back row: Nichols, T. Spencer, T. Knight. Middle row: Tyler, Captain W.C. Hedley, V.T. Hill, W.N. Roe, Reverend A.P. Wickham, H.E. Murray-Anderdon. Front row: C.J. Robinson, S.M.J. Woods, L.C.H. Palairet, H.T. Hewett, (Captain), G. Fowler, A.E. Newton, J.B. Challen.

SOMERSET v. YORKSHIRE.

PLAYED AT

TAUNTON, THURSDAY & FRIDAY, August 25th and 26th, 1892.

Draw (Rain).

YORKSHIRE.

First Innings.

Mr. E. Smith (Capt.)	b Tyler	..	45
Mr. F. S. Jackson	run out	..	55
Tunnicliffe	l b w, b Tyler	..	30
Mr. A. Sellers	c Hewett, b Tyler	..	29
Ulyett	b Hedley	..	6
Peel	c Nichols, b Tyler	..	47
Wainwright	st Palairet, b Tyler	..	43
Wardall	c Hill, b Tyler	..	14
Brown	not out	..	12
Moorhouse	c Woods, b Tyler	..	11
Ellis	b Nichols	..	0
	B 7	..	7
	Total		299

SOMERSET.

First Innings.

Mr. H. T. Hewett (Capt.)	b Peel	..	201
Mr. L. C. H. Palairet	c Sellers, b Jackson	..	146
Mr. J. B. Challen	b Peel	..	6
Mr. W. C. Hedley	c Wardall, b Peel	..	102
Mr. A. E. Newton	c Sellers, b Jackson	..	4
Mr. V. T. Hill	c Brown, b Peel	..	39
Mr. S. M. J. Woods	c Wardall, b Wainwright	..	31
Mr. G. Fowler	not out	..	32
Nichols	c Sellers, b Peel	..	7
Mr. C. J. Robinson	st Ellis, b Peel	..	2
Tyler	b Peel	..	1
	B 19, l-b 2	..	21
	Total		*592

BOWLING ANALYSIS.

YORKSHIRE—1st Innings.

		O.	M.	R.	W.
Tyler	..	50	13	111	7
Nichols	..	22·4	7	62	1
Mr. Hedley	..	28	6	67	1
Mr. Woods	..	19	7	52	0

SOMERSET—1st Innings.

	O.	M.	R.	W.		O.	M.	R.	W.
Jackson	39	8	148	2	Wardall	9	1	35	0
Peel	60·3	16	133	7	Brown	2	0	8	0
Wainwright	33	6	117	1	Ulyett	3	0	12	0
Smith	23	2	97	0	Moorhouse	5	1	21	0

* Highest Aggregate Innings in 1892.

Umpires—C. K. Pullin & J. Lillywhite.   Scorers—T. H. Knight & H. Turner.

LANCASHIRE

15, 16, 17 July 1895 at Taunton

The fact that Somerset lost by an innings and 452 runs was overshadowed by the record-breaking innings of 424 made by the Lancashire captain, A.C. MacLaren. Aged just twenty-three, he exceeded the previous first-class record of 344, held by W.G. Grace, and in batting for 470 minutes, he also played the longest recorded innings. He gave his first chance when he had scored 262 and his innings included just 1 six, a hit right out of the ground, but he was to reach the boundary on no fewer than 62 occasions. His four 100s were scored in rapid fashion, in 155 minutes, 105 minutes, 90 and 94 minutes!

It could have been a totally different story if the first ball of the match, delivered by Ted Tyler, had not missed the stumps by the narrowest of margins. MacLaren's opening partner, Ward, was the first to reach 50, but by then MacLaren was in full flow, batting superbly with shots all around the wicket, most of which seemed to arrive at the boundary.

The Somerset bowlers stuck to their task, with Tyler bowling 59 overs. Wood 46 and L.C.H. Palairet had his longest spell with 44 overs even though they were only five-ball overs in 1895. When the time came for Somerset to bat, exhaustion could well be the excuse for a poor first innings score of 143 and though they fared slightly better in the second innings, scoring 206, it was not sufficient to make Lancashire bat again.

The match is quite remarkable in terms of the records that were broken: the highest individual score – 424; the highest innings score – 801; the longest innings – 470 minutes; and the largest victory/defeat – an innings and 452 runs!

A.C. MacLaren.

SOMERSET *v.* LANCASHIRE

Played on the County Ground, Taunton, 15, 16 and 17 July, 1895

LANCASHIRE WON BY AN INNINGS AND 452 RUNS

LANCASHIRE	FIRST INNINGS	
*Mr A.C. MacLaren	c Fowler b Gamlin	424
A. Ward	c R.C.N. Palairet b Tyler	64
A.G. Paul	c Gamlin b L.C.H. Palairet	177
A.W. Hallam	c Fowler b L.C.H. Palairet	6
Mr C.H. Benton	c and b Fowler	43
F.H. Sugg	c Wickham b Woods	41
A. Tinsley	c Gamlin b Woods	0
G.R. Baker	st Wickham b L.C.H. Palairet	23
J. Briggs	not out	9
†C. Smith	c Trask b L.C.H. Palairet	0
A.W. Mold	c R.C.N. Palairet b Gamlin	0
Extras	b 9, lb 4, w 1	14
Total		801

Fall: 1-141 2-504 3-530 4-637 5-732 6-738 7-792 8-792 9-798

BOWLING	O	M	R	W
Tyler	59	5	212	1
Woods	46	5	163	2
L.C.H. Palairet	44	10	133	4
Gamlin	26	8	100	2
Fowler	23	5	97	1
R.C.N. Palairet	11	3	41	0
Trask	2	0	9	0
Porch	5	3	16	0
Bartlett	6	0	16	0

SOMERSET	FIRST INNINGS		SECOND INNINGS	
Mr L.C.H. Palairet	b Briggs	30	b Mold	4
Mr G. Fowler	c sub b Hallam	39	(6) c MacLaren b Mold	46
Mr R.C.N. Palairet	c Hallam b Mold	2	(4) st Smith b Briggs	7
Mr H.T. Stanley	c Smith b Briggs	8	(3) c Smith b Mold	12
Mr R.B. Porch	run out	18	(7) c MacLaren b Mold	1
*Mr S.M.J. Woods	c Smith b Mold	11	(5) b Briggs	55
Dr J.E. Trask	c Ward b Mold	11	(8) c and b Mold	26
†Rev A.P. Wickham	b Mold	3	(10) not out	0
E.J. Tyler	not out	15	(2) b Briggs	41
Mr E.W. Bartlett	b Briggs	4	(9) c Mold b Briggs	6
H.T. Gamlin	st Smith b Briggs	0	hit wkt b Briggs	0
Extras	leg byes	2	b 4, lb 4	8
Total		143		206

Fall: 1st inns: 1-71 2-73 3-73 4-94 5-107 6-121 7-122 8-132 9-137
     2nd inns: 1-5 2-61 3-61 4-83 5-150 6-151 7-187 8-206 9-206

BOWLING	O	M	R	W	O	M	R	W
Briggs	37.3	15	59	4	37	17	78	5
Mold	35	15	75	4	33	11	76	5
Hallam	2	1	7	1	8	2	19	0
Baker					5	2	25	0

Umpires: J. Wickens and G. Hay.

Lancashire won the toss. Close of play: 1st day: Lancashire 555-3 (MacLaren 289*, Benton 6*); 2nd day: Somerset (2) 58-1 (Tyler 38*, Stanley 12*).

* Captain; † Wicket-keeper

SURREY

22, 23, 24 August 1895 at Taunton

Surrey, the County Champions, had defeated Somerset at the Oval earlier in the season by 9 wickets – even though Sammy Woods had taken 7 wickets in their first innings – and Somerset were keen to get their revenge.

The return at Taunton was again a low-scoring match, with Somerset struggling to 168 in their first innings, thankful for a fine 64 from L.C.H. Palairet. Richardson, who was later to play one game for Somerset, did most of the damage by taking 6 wickets.

Surrey fared even worse when it was their turn to bat, entirely due to the slow bowling of Ted Tyler. Opening the bowling as he often did, with Sammy Woods at the other end, he bowled 34.3 overs, yielding only 49 runs and achieved the rare feat of taking all 10 wickets in an innings. Two good catches by Hedley helped get rid of the opening pair, Abel and Read (M.), but after a determined 34 from Hayward, the rest of the Surrey batsmen had no answer to the wiles of Tyler and the side was dismissed for 139.

Batting for a second time Somerset again struggled, this time to 131 after L.C.H. Palairet and Fowler had given them a fair start. It was the fast bowling of Richardson that proved too good for the majority of the batsmen, and his figures of 7 for 67 were well deserved as were his match figures of 13 for 152.

Surrey never looked like scoring the 170 required for victory, althought this time Tyler had to be satisfied with only 3 wickets. Somerset were further helped by Surrey's poor running between the wickets which resulted in three runs out. No batsman looked comfortable and an innings of 117 left Somerset the victors by 53 runs – sweet revenge for the defeat at the Oval.

Ted Tyler.

L.C.H. Palairet.

SOMERSET v. SURREY

PLAYED AT

TAUNTON, Thursday, Friday and Saturday, August 22nd, 23rd and 24th, 1895.

Won by 53 Runs.

SOMERSET.

	First Innings.		Second Innings.	
Mr. G. Fowler	b Richardson	20	b Richardson	44
Mr. L. C. H. Palairet	c Marshall b Lockwood	64	c Marshall b Richardson	26
Mr. W. N. Roe	c W. Read b Richardson	0	b Lohmann	6
Mr. C. E. Dunlop	c Lockwood b Lohmann	7	c Lohmann b Richardson	33
Capt. W. C. Hedley	b Lohmann	1	l-b-w b Lohmann	8
Mr. S. M. J. Woods	c Marshall b Richardson	26	c Marshall b Richardson	2
Smith (W.)	b Lockwood	7	b Richardson	1
Nichols	b Richardson	15	c Lohmann b Richardson	4
Mr. A. E. Newton	b Richardson	14	c Richardson b Lohmann	1
Westcott	c Marshall b Richardson	0	not out	2
Tyler	not out	5	c and b Richardson	13
	B 5, l-b 4	9	B 1	1
	Total	168	Total	141

SURREY.

	First Innings.		Second Innings.	
Abel	c Hedley b Tyler	34	run out	16
Read (M.)	c Hedley b Tyler	21	c Newton b Woods	15
Hayward	c Palairet b Tyler	34	b Hedley	12
Brockwell	b Tyler	4	c Palairet b Tyler	27
Holland	c Dunlop b Tyler	13	l-b-w b Tyler	11
Mr. W. W. Read	b Tyler	8	run out	1
Lockwood	not out	11	c Wood b Tyler	7
H. D. G. Leveson-Gower	l-b-w b Tyler	0	run out	3
Lohmann	c and b Tyler	0	not out	5
Marshall	c Newton b Tyler	6	c and b Hedley	10
Richardson	b Tyler	4	b Hedley	10
	B 4	4		
	Total	139	Total	117

BOWLING ANALYSIS.

SOMERSET.	First Innings.				Second Innings.			
	O.	M.	R.	W.	O.	M.	R.	W.
Lohmann	15	3	46	2	23	6	52	3
Lockwood	11	4	28	2	5	1	21	0
Richardson	25.4	4	85	6	29	8	67	7

SURREY.	First Innings.				Second Innings.			
	O.	M.	R.	W.	O.	M.	R.	W.
Mr. S. M. J. Woods	18	7	44	0	10	1	32	1
Tyler	34.3	15	49	10	32	15	42	3
Nichols	14	4	28	0	—	—	—	—
Capt. W C. Hedley	3	1	14	0	22.2	6	43	3

Umpires—J. Wickens and W. J. Collishaw.   Scorers—T. H. Knight and F. Boyington.

YORKSHIRE

15, 16, 17 July 1901 at Leeds

Ten years after being admitted to the County Championship, Somerset were still relying on amateurs. Whilst they were fortunate in having two or three exceptionally good ones, many of the others were not even good club cricketers.

For the journey north to take on the Champions, Yorkshire, even finding eleven players proved to be difficult and at the last moment Mr G. Burrington, a godson of Sammy Woods, was drafted into the team.

Sammy Woods won the toss and elected to bat on a lively and indifferent wicket. A decision that was soon regretted when two of Somerset's stars, Mr L.C.H. Palairet and Len Braund, were both dismissed without scoring. V.T. Hill, Robson and Newton also failed to trouble the scorers, and Somerset were somewhat fortunate to reach 87 with Wilfred Rhodes taking 5 wickets.

There was a glimmer of hope when Yorkshire's premier batsman also failed and with the all-rounders, Hirst, Rhodes and Haigh, still to come Yorkshire reached 325. This was thought to be a winning total, but Somerset had other ideas.

The ever confident Sammy Woods wagered that Palairet would score a century and he even had the courage to take long odds on a Somerset victory – would he be proved a wise man or a fool?

The opening pair, Palairet and Braund, certainly made up for their first innings failure, each scoring a century – much to Sammy's delight – and Palairet went on to score 173. A century by Phillips plus sound contributions from Woods, Hill and Robson saw Somerset total a remarkable 630 from a tired and dispirited Yorkshire attack. By the close of play on the second day, Somerset had reached 549 for 5 and all Yorkshire could do was to pray for rain.

Their prayers were not answered and they were left to score 393 to win. It soon ceased to be a contest. Cranfield and Braund took 4 wickets each and ensured a victory by 279 runs, with the happiest man in England, Sammy Woods, counting his winnings.

Sammy Woods.

W. Rhodes.

L.C.H. Palairet.

L.C. Braund.

SOMERSET v. YORKSHIRE.

PLAYED AT

LEEDS, Monday, Tuesday and Wednesday, July 15th, 16th and 17th, 1901.

Won by 279 runs.

SOMERSET.

	First Innings.		Second Innings.	
Mr. L. C. H. Palairet	b Hirst	0	c and b Brown	173
Braund	b Rhodes	0	b Haigh	107
Lewis	c Tunnicliffe b Rhodes	10	b Rhodes	12
Mr. F. A. Phillips	b Hirst	12	b Wainwright	122
Mr. S. M. J. Woods	c Hunter b Haigh	46	c Tunnicliffe b Hirst	66
Mr. V. T. Hill	run out	0	c Hirst b Rhodes	53
Robson	c Hunter b Rhodes	0	c Tunnicliffe b Rhodes	40
Gill	c Hunter b Rhodes	4	st Hunter b Rhodes	14
Mr. A. E. Newton	b Haigh	0	c Taylor b Rhodes	4
Mr. G. Burrington	c Brown b Rhodes	11	st Hunter b Rhodes	15
Cranfield	not out	1	not out	5
	B 2, l-b 1	3	B 16, n-b 3	19
	Total	87	Total	630

YORKSHIRE.

	First Innings.		Second Innings.	
Brown	c Braund b Cranfield	24	c sub b Gill	5
Tunnicliffe	c Newton b Gill	9	c Palairet b Braund	44
Denton	c Woods b Gill	12	b Braund	16
Mr. T. L. Taylor	b Cranfield	1	absent hurt	0
Mr. F. Mitchell	b Gill	4	b Braund	21
Hirst	c Robson b Cranfield	61	l-b-w b Braund	6
Wainwright	b Gill	9	c Lewis b Cranfield	1
Lord Hawke	b Robson	37	c Burrington b Cranfield	4
Haigh	c Robson b Cranfield	96	not out	2
Rhodes	c Lewis b Robson	44	st Newton b Cranfield	0
Hunter	not out	10	c Woods b Cranfield	0
	B 13, w 5	18	B 12, n-b 2	14
	Total	325	Total	113

BOWLING ANALYSIS.

SOMERSET.

	First Innings.				Second Innings.			
	O.	M.	R.	W.	O.	M.	R.	W.
Hirst	12	5	36	2	37	1	189	1
Rhodes	16	8	39	5	46.5	12	145	6
Haigh	4	—	9	2	20	4	78	1
Wainwright	—	—	—	—	34	3	107	1
Brown	—	—	—	—	18	1	92	1

Hirst bowled three no-balls.

YORKSHIRE.

	First Innings.				Second Innings.			
	O.	M.	R.	W.	O.	M.	R.	W.
Cranfield	27	5	113	4	18	5	35	4
Gill	23	2	105	4	4	1	23	1
Braund	5	—	33	—	15	3	41	4
Robson	10	1	35	2	—	—	—	—
Mr. Woods	5	1	21	—	—	—	—	—
Mr. Palairet	1	1	—	—	—	—	—	—

Cranfield bowled five wides. Gill and Braund each bowled one no-ball.

Umpires—W. Wright and T. Mycroft.

YORKSHIRE
16, 17, 18 June 1902 at Sheffield

The venue in 1901 had been Leeds, but the change to Sheffield in 1902 did not alter the result, with Somerset winning once again, this time by 34 runs. It proved to be Yorkshire's only defeat in the Championship and, whilst the high scoring of the previous year was not repeated – in fact, it was a low-scoring match – the excitement was even greater.

Somerset won the toss and decided to bat; 44 runs were scored by the two openers, L.C.H. Palairet and Braund, and this was considered to be satisfactory given that the pitch was far from reliable. After lunch it was a very different story, Rhodes and Jackson demolished the Somerset batting and only a further 42 runs were added, with Rhodes taking 4 for 39 and Jackson doing even better with 6 for 29.

The Somerset bowlers now showed their worth. Other than Denton and Brown, the rest of the Yorkshire batting was very poor, being completely overcome, and they were fortunate to attain a meagre 74 runs. What Rhodes and Jackson could do, Braund and Robson could do even better, with the former taking 6 for 30 and the latter 3 for 2. They had achieved a lead of just 12, but how vital these runs would prove to be for Somerset.

The weather then decided to play its part and no cricket was possible on the second day. Somerset had to wait until lunchtime on the final day before starting their second innings. Palairet and Braund repeated their first-innings success, but only Gill of the later batsmen reached double figures. His hard-hit 41 helped the score along to 106 but not before Haigh took a 'hat-trick' – he actually took the last 5 wickets without conceding a run.

Yorkshire needed 119 runs to win but Braund, this time with the ball, made their task impossible with some superb bowling. His final analysis was 9 for 41 and only Tunnicliffe and T.L. Taylor reached double figures. A final total of 84 left Somerset the victors for the second year running – this time by 34 runs.

S. Haigh.

SOMERSET v. YORKSHIRE

PLAYED AT

SHEFFIELD, Monday, Tuesday and Wednesday, June 16th, 17th and 18th, 1902.

Won by 34 Runs.

SOMERSET.

	First Innings.			Second Innings.	
Mr. L. C. H. Palairet	b Jackson	25	c and b Jackson		24
Braund	c and b Rhodes	31	c Jackson b Haigh		34
Robson	b Jackson	o	b Jackson		o
Mr. P. R. Johnson	b Jackson	o	run out		3
Mr. S. M. J. Woods	l-b-w b Rhodes	14	c Hirst b Rhodes		o
Lewis	c Haigh b Rhodes	1	b Haigh		4
Gill	l-b-w b Jackson	1	b Haigh		41
Mr. F. M. Lee	c Denton b Rhodes	1	b Haigh		o
Mr. A. E. Newton	b Jackson	o	b Haigh		o
Cranfield	b Jackson	5	not out		o
Mr. D. L. Evans	not out	6	b Haigh		o
	l-b 1, n-b 1	2			
	Total	86		Total	106

YORKSHIRE.

	First Innings.			Second Innings.	
Brown	b Cranfield	13	c Johnson b Cranfield		6
Tunnicliffe	b Braund	4	c Robson b Braund		11
Denton	b Robson	20	b Braund		6
Mr. T. L. Taylor	c Newton b Braund	8	st Newton b Braund		18
Mr. F. S. Jackson	b Braund	5	b Braund		8
Hirst	c Evans b Braund	o	c Palairet b Braund		9
Washington	b Robson	o	b Braund		3
Haigh	b Braund	9	b Braund		6
Rhodes	b Braund	5	c and b Braund		5
Lord Hawke	l-b-w b Robson	1	b Braund		6
Hunter	not out	1	not out		o
	B 5, l-b 3	8	B 4, l-b 2		6
	Total	74		Total	84

BOWLING ANALYSIS.

SOMERSET.

	First Innings.				Second Innings.			
	O.	M.	R.	W.	O.	M.	R.	W.
Hirst	7	3	8	o	2	o	5	o
Rhodes	26	10	39	4	12	o	44	1
Mr. Jackson	24.2	12	29	6	21	7	38	2
Haigh	4	2	8	o	7.1	1	19	6

Hirst bowled a no-ball.

YORKSHIRE.

	First Innings.				Second Innings.			
	O.	M.	R.	W.	O.	M.	R.	W.
Cranfield	7	o	34	1	9	o	22	1
Braund	13	2	30	6	17.3	5	41	9
Robson	6	5	2	3	9	3	15	o

Umpires—G. Porter and W. Wright.

THE AUSTRALIANS

13, 14, 15 July 1905 at Bath

The Australians brought a very strong team to Bath and their batsmen took full advantage of the good batting conditions, even though some time was lost because of rain.

On the first day they scored 469 for the loss of Trumper, but not before he had scored a delightful 86 out of an opening partnership of 145, and Hill for just 11. This brought in Noble to join a rampant Armstrong, who looked capable of batting for the whole three days.

On a previous tour in 1899, Trumper had scored the first ever 300 by an Australian in England and it seemed certain that Armstrong was keen to beat this record. At the close of play on the first day he was 252*; although he was extremely cautious when he resumed play on the second day, as expected, he reached his target and was 303* when the declaration finally came. He had batted in glorious style through his long innings, hitting a six and 38 fours in an innings lasting 375 minutes. His third-wicket stand with Noble yielded 320 runs, scored in 200 minutes, before Noble was caught by Poyntz off Woods for 127.

Armstrong was dropped twice, but not before he had scored 200. Noble's innings was without blemish – not a chance was given, even though Somerset tried 10 bowlers.

With no hope of winning and little hope of even saving the game, Somerset had their own hero in Len Braund. He scored 117 before falling to the Armstrong/Noble combination. By the close of play on the second day they had reached 188 for 4, but on the final morning wickets fell rapidly and they were all out for 228, with Cotter and Noble each taking 4 wickets.

Following-on with only one aim in view – to bat for the rest of the day – Somerset changed their batting order and opened with H. Martyn and Len Braund. Was it inspired captaincy? They put on 146 before Braund was out but Martyn went on to score his first ever 100. In fact it was to be his only first-class 100 in his long career but it certainly saved the day, Somerset ending with 254 for 4.

Over 1,100 runs were scored in under 800 minutes – the match was a real feast for the many supporters.

Warwick Armstrong.

A. Lewis.

SOMERSET v. THE AUSTRALIANS

PLAYED AT
BATH, Thursday, Friday and Saturday, July 13th, 14th and 15th, 1905.

Drawn.

AUSTRALIANS.
First Innings.

Mr. V. T. Trumper	... c Palairet b Robson ...	86
Mr. W. W. Armstrong	... not out ...	303
Mr. C. Hill	... c Woods b Braund ...	11
Mr. M. A. Noble	... c Poyntz b Woods ...	127
Mr. R. A. Duff	... c Newton b Robson ...	12
Mr. J. Darling	... not out ...	49
Mr. D. R. A. Gehrs		
Mr. C. E. McLeod		
Mr. A. Cotter	} did not bat.	
Mr. F. Laver		
Mr. J. J. Kelly		

B 16, l-b 4, w 1   ... 21

Total (for 4 wickets) *609

*Innings declared closed.

SOMERSET.

	First Innings.		Second Innings.	
Mr. L. C. H. Palairet	... b Cotter	... 4	not out	... 2
L. C. Braund	... c Armstrong b Noble	... 117	c sub. b Laver	... 62
A. Lewis	... c Darling b Noble	... 11	b Armstrong	... 17
Mr. H. S. Poyntz	... run out	... 6	c Duff b McLeod	... 11
E. Robson	... c Armstrong b McLeod	42		
Mr. H. Martyn	... c Darling b Cotter	... 22	not out	... 130
Mr. S. M. J. Woods	... b Cotter	... 1		
W. Montgomery	... b Cotter	... 1	c sub. b McLeod	... 11
Mr. A. E. Newton	... c Laver b Noble	... 4		
T. Richardson	... not out	... 4		
Mr. J. Thomas	... b Noble	... 0		

B 10, l-b 2, w 3, n-b 1   16   B   ... 21

Total   ... 228   Total (for 4 wickets) 254

BOWLING ANALYSIS.
AUSTRALIANS—First Innings.

	O.	M.	R.	W.
Braund	... 34	2	142	1
Mr. Thomas	... 14	1	65	0
Robson	... 36	6	114	2
Richardson	... 13	1	65	0
Mr. Palairet	... 11	1	48	0
Montgomery	... 13	1	43	0
Mr. Woods	... 15	0	64	1
Mr. Poyntz	... 4	0	25	0
Mr. Martyn	... 3	0	22	0

Mr. Palairet bowled a wide.

SOMERSET. First Innings. | Second Innings.

	O.	M.	R.	W.	O.	M.	R.	W.
Mr. Cotter	... 24	5	101	4	7	0	50	0
Mr. Noble	... 23.4	10	45	4	8	2	21	0
Mr. McLeod	... 16	5	31	1	13	4	49	2
Mr. Laver	... 12	3	23	0	15	2	53	1
Mr. Armstrong	... 5	1	12	0	19	9	39	1
Mr. Duff	... —	—	—	—	4	0	21	0

Mr. Noble bowled 1 no ball and 2 wides,
and Mr. Laver 1 wide.

Umpires—S. Brown and A. A. White.

GLOUCESTERSHIRE

4, 5, 6 July 1907 at Bristol

Owing to rain, this match was reduced to little over one day's play, but it nevertheless provided a great deal of excitement for both players and spectators. No play at all was possible on the first day and there was only sufficient time for Gloucestershire to score 50 for the loss of 2 wickets, with Langdon scoring an aggressive 40 on the second. What would the third day bring?

Further rain during the night and a wet Saturday morning made play extremely doubtful and the pitch was getting worse by the minute, but both captains were determined to play, each hoping for an unlikely victory.

Without the aid of 'freak' declarations, what was in effect a one-day game was played with both sides striving to gain the upper hand. Gloucestershire continued to bat and reached 139 for 5 before declaring, with Braund taking three of the wickets.

Somerset got off to a dreadful start and found themselves 14 for 5 but Woods and Robson, batting late in the order, succeeded in taking the score to 76 – Dennett had the excellent figures of 6 for 37. Gloucestershire, sensing a sensational victory, then declared at 47 for 4 – Braund 2 for 14, leaving Somerset 75 minutes to score 115 to win.

Again the challenge was met with 54 runs scored in 40 minutes, but with the loss of 6 wickets and only 35 minutes left and 61 runs still needed, Gloucestershire appeared to be the more likely winners. C.G. Deane, in his first season with Somerset, defended bravely and with help from the 'tail', somehow prevented a Gloucestershire victory. When stumps were drawn Somerset still needed 13 runs with 2 wickets remaining, but all credit to the two captains, G.L. Jessop and Sammy Woods, for making possible such an exciting final day. Even Sammy was pleased with this draw!

G.L. Jessop.

G. Dennett.

GLOUCESTERSHIRE.

H. Wrathall c Palairet b Lewis	2	— b Braund	11
T. Langdon b Robson	68	— b Lewis	19
J. H. Board b Braund	8	— run out	5
A. Winstone b Braund	17		
Mr. G. L. Jessop c Lewis b Braund	5	— b Braund	4
Mr. F. M. Luce not out	23	— not out	2
Capt. C. E. B. Champain not out	3		
B 9, l-b 4	13	B 4, l-b 2	6
	*139		*47

*Innings declared closed.

Mr. E. Barnett ⎱
P. Mill   ⎰
Parker   ⎱ did not bat.
G. Dennett ⎰

SOMERSET.

Mr. L. C. H. Palairet st Board b Dennett	4	— c Mills b Dennett	4
L. C. Braund c Jessop b Dennett	2	— lbw b Dennett	2
Mr. B. L. Bisgood b Parker	1	— c Wrathall b Dennett	17
A. E. Lewis c Board b Dennett	0	— b Dennett	8
Mr. C. G. Deane st Board b Dennett	0	— not out	24
Mr. G. W. Jupp c Jessop b Dennett	7	— b Jessop	5
Mr. S. M. J. Woods b Mills	18	— c Langdon b Jessop	29
E. Robson b Mills	13	— b Jessop	2
Mr. E. S. M. Poyntz st Board b Dennett	4	— st Board b Dennett	0
Mr. A. E. Newton not out	3		
A. E. Bailey c Wrathall b Jessop	12		
B 4, l-b 3, w 1	8	B 9, l-b 2	11
	72		102

SOMERSET BOWLING.

	Overs	Mdns.	Runs	Wkts.	Overs	Mdns.	Runs	Wkts.
Lewis	8	3	17	1	0.1	0	0	1
Bailey	4	1	19	0				
Braund	20	5	57	3	4	1	14	2
Robson	16	5	32	1	.3	0	27	0
Jupp	1	0	1	0				

GLOUCESTERSHIRE BOWLING.

	Overs	Mdns.	Runs	Wkts.	Overs	Mdns.	Runs	Wkts.
Dennett	16	6	37	6	16.5	4	34	5
Parker	8	2	15	1				
Mills	6	1	8	2	5	0	20	0
Jessop	2	0	4	1	11	2	37	3

Umpires: A. A. White and C. E. Dench.

Courtesy of Wisden Cricketers' Almanack.

MIDDLESEX

20, 21, 22 May 1907 at Lord's

This is a match that will always be talked about and will remain in the record books for all time.

Albert Trott chose it for his benefit and it was expected to be a typical County game between two fairly strong sides with prominent amateurs filling no less than 13 of the 22 places.

Rain interrupted play on the first day, but Middlesex were still able to score 286 against good bowling by Lewis and Mordaunt, Pelham Warner and Tarrant had got them off to a good start, but wickets fell at regular intervals with no batsmen really dominating play.

Conditions were only slightly better on the second day, but some poor Middlesex fielding helped Somerset reach 236, leaving a deficit of 50. It was fourth change bowler, Tarrant, that did the damage taking 6 for 47 but Len Braund, opening the innings, made up for his lack of success as a bowler by scoring a valuable 59.

Middlesex were keen to extend their lead as quickly as possible, and in doing so lost early wickets, but a stand by Littlejohn and Trott steadied the ship and they finally saw their total reach 213, leaving Somerset needing 264 to win.

However, the real drama was still to come. Palairet and Braund found little difficulty in scoring against the opening bowlers. Palairet scored a delightful 35 before being caught by Bosanquet off Tarrant and shortly afterwards, history was made. Trott only needed to bowl 8 overs in taking 7 wickets, which included 4 in consecutive balls and a further hat-trick. He took the wickets of Lewis lbw and then clean-bowled Poyntz, Woods and Robinson, also catching Johnson and Lee off the bowling of Tarrant before ending the innings by dismissing Mordaunt, Wickham and Bailey with consecutive balls.

Trott's 7 for 20 demolished Somerset, who could only total 97 and lost by 166 runs, although they did enter the record books – even if it was for the wrong reason.

A.E. Trott.

E. Robson.

MIDDLESEX.

Mr. P. F. Warner b Mordaunt .... 46 — b Lewis 11
F. A. Tarrant c Lee b Lewis .... 52 — c Palairet b Mordaunt 28
Mr. G. W. Beldam lbw, b Mordaunt...... 12 — lbw, b Lewis................. 0
Mr. B. J. T. Bosanquet c Johnson b Mor-
   daunt .... 32 — b Bailey 29
Mr. E. S. Litteljohn c Braund b Lewis .. 44 — b Mordaunt 52
A. E. Trott b Lewis .... 1 — c Wickham b Robson........ 35
Mr. H. A. Milton b Lewis .... 3 — b Mordaunt 0
Mr. G. MacGregor c Woods b Bailey .... 39 — c Poyntz b Robson.......... 39
H. R. Murrell b Robson .... 33 — c and b Braund 9
J. T. Hearne not out.................. 3 — not out 4
E. Mignon b Bailey .... 1 — c Wickham b Braund........ 0
    B 15, l-b 4, n-b 1.................. 20   B 3, l-b 2, n-b 1 6
                                  —
                              286   213

SOMERSET.

Mr. L. C. H. Palairet c MacGregor b Mignon 6 — c Bosanquet b Tarrant 35
L. C. Braund c MacGregor b Bosanquet .. 59 — not out 28
Mr. P. R. Johnson b Tarrant .... 57 — c Trott b Tarrant 14
A. E. Lewis c Tarrant b Mignon .... 31 — lbw, b Trott 1
Mr. E. S. M. Poyntz lbw, b Tarrant..... 9 — b Trott 0
Mr. S. M. J. Woods c Bosanquet b Tarrant 17 — b Trott 0
E. Robson not out.................... 20 — b Trott 0
Mr. F. M. Lee b Hearne ... . 18 — c Trott b Tarrant 7
Mr. O. C. Mordaunt c Beldam b Tarrant.. 1 — c Mignon b Trott........... 4
Rev. A. P. Wickham c Trott b Tarrant .. 0 — b Trott 0
A. E. Bailey c Litteljohn b Tarrant ...... 3 — c Mignon b Trott 0
    L-b 14, w 1 15   B 4, l-b 4 8
                                  —
                              236   97

SOMERSET BOWLING.

	Overs	Mdns.	Runs	Wkts.	Overs	Mdns.	Runs	Wkts.
Lewis	32	14	88	4	7	2	17	2
Bailey	16	5	33	2	16	3	58	1
Braund	13	1	33	0	13.4	1	55	2
Mordaunt	30	6	97	3	15	1	47	3
Robson	7	1	15	1	6	2	30	2

MIDDLESEX BOWLING.

	Overs	Mdns.	Runs	Wkts.	Overs	Mdns.	Runs	Wkts.
Beldam	4	1	15	0	3	1	10	0
Mignon	24	6	88	2	5	1	24	0
Trott	5	1	10	0	8	2	20	7
Hearne	8	1	22	1				
Bosanquet	8	0	39	1				
Tarrant	15	4	47	6	14		35	3

Umpires : F. W. Marlow and S. Brown.

Courtesy of Wisden Cricketers' Almanack.

Hampshire

10, 11, 12 August 1908 at Southampton

This was a Somerset victory against all the odds, as Hampshire had scored 425 in their first innings with contributions from all their batsmen, Mr A.J.L. Hill being their highest scorer with a painstaking 80. Only Robson of the Somerset bowlers really looked dangerous, although both Greswell and Lewis gave him good support.

Had it not been for a fine innings by P.R. Johnson, Somerset would have been in dire straits. His 117 enabled them to reach 262 but only V.T. Hill gave him real support.

While Hampshire were in a position to enforce the follow-on, they declined to do so and perhaps regretted it when Greswell, bowling superbly, took 7 wickets for 42 from 15.4 overs. Hampshire's second innings folded for only 128 runs with a top score of 32 from the opening batsman, Bowell.

Even this small total left Somerset with the daunting task of scoring 292 to win on a wicket that had already begun to break up. This apparently impossible task was met by some of the best batting seen for years, and the last day was an education in the art of scoring runs. Three wickets, Johnson, Bisgood and Lewis, fell for 93, which still left 199 to get, with playing time fast running out.

Sammy Woods' well-known aversion for draws may well have helped create one of Somerset's finest victories. With Len Braund they played an array of incredible shots, thrilling spectators and players alike, and Sammy reached his first century in three years, with Len Braund's magnificent 124* all scored on a pitch which if anything was favourable to the bowlers.

The Woods-Braund partnership was a record for the fourth wicket against Hampshire and remained so until it was equalled by Walford (264) and Lawrence (67) at Weston-Super-Mare in 1947.

P.R. Johnson.

L.C. Braund

HAMPSHIRE.

Batsman	1st Innings		2nd Innings	
Mr. A. C. Johnston b Robson	40	—	c Chidgey b Lewis	5
A. Bowell c Johnston b Braund	65	—	c Chidgey b Lewis	32
C. B. Llewellyn b Greswell	17	—	b Greswell	13
P. Mead c V. T. Hill b Braund	41	—	b Greswell	23
Mr. A. J. L. Hill c Lewis b V. T. Hill	80	—	b Lewis	4
Mr. A. J. Evans b Robson	48	—	lbw, b Greswell	18
Mr. G. N. Bignell c Whittle b Robson	44	—	b Greswell	0
A. Stone c Chidgey b Robson	12	—	c Bisgood b Greswell	12
E. R. Remnant b Greswell	16	—	not out	7
J. Newman not out	34	—	c and b Greswell	0
J. R. Badcock c Braund b Lewis	2	—	b Greswell	8
B 17, l-b 8, n-b 1	26		B 4, w 1, n-b 1	6
	425			**128**

SOMERSET.

Batsman	1st Innings		2nd Innings	
Mr. P. R. Johnson c Mead b Newman	117	—	b Newman	19
A. E. Lewis c Stone b Badcock	16	—	c Mead b Badcock	3
A. E. Whittle st Stone b Llewellyn	2			
Mr. B. L. Bisgood c Stone b Llewellyn	17	—	b Mead	19
L. C. Braund c Evans b Llewellyn	29	—	not out	124
Mr. V. T. Hill c Bowell b Newman	41			
E. Robson b Llewellyn	0			
Mr. S. M. J. Woods c Johnston b Badcock	18	—	not out	105
Mr. M. M. Munden c Mead b Badcock	9			
H. Chidgey b Newman	1			
Mr. W. T. Greswell not out	0			
B 4, w 4, n-b 4	12		B 11, l-b 6, n-b 4	22
	262			**292**

SOMERSET BOWLING.

	Overs	Mdns.	Runs	Wkts.		Overs	Mdns.	Runs	Wkts.
Greswell	30	6	89	2	....	15.4	3	42	7
Lewis	35	11	103	1	....	15	2	61	3
Robson	31	7	107	4	....	4	1	19	0
V. T. Hill	7	1	44	1					
Braund	21	5	56	2					

HAMPSHIRE BOWLING.

	Overs	Mdns.	Runs	Wkts.		Overs	Mdns.	Runs	Wkts.
Badcock	16	1	79	3	....	18.2	3	93	1
Mead	16	3	56	0	....	17	5	40	1
Llewellyn	10	1	50	4	....	11	1	41	0
Newman	13.1	4	30	3	....	25	6	54	1
Evans	3	0	18	0	....	3	1	10	0
Bignell	2	0	10	0					
A. J. L. Hill	1	0	7	0	....	3	1	6	0
Remnant						7	0	26	0

Umpires : W. A. J. West and F. Parris.

Courtesy of Wisden Cricketers' Almanack.

WORCESTERSHIRE
26, 27, 28 June 1913 at Worcester

It must be frustrating to score 257* and be on the losing side by such a large margin as eight wickets, but this was the fate of Len Braund in the match at Worcester. Finding his way to the crease after Somerset had lost two quick wickets, he was soon at his imperial best. Dropped in the slips with his score on 34, he then proceeded to play one of the all-time great innings of Somerset's relatively short history. He took only 45 minutes to register his first 50, his century came in 130 minutes and it took him just over a further hour to get to his 200. In all he scored 257* in 225 minutes, with 35 fours out of 370 runs scored whilst he was batting. The only other worthwhile contribution to the score was 41 by Hyman, and Burrows and Pearson both took 4 wickets for Worcestershire.

Somerset were feeling very pleased with their 383 and even more so when Worcestershire wickets began to fall to White. It was not until their number eight came to the wicket that things began to change. This number eight was Frank Chester, later to become a leading umpire, who went on to score his first County century, and showed real promise, that was sadly ended by the First World War. His 115 lifted Worcestershire to within 39 runs of Somerset's total.

Second time around, Somerset found batting much more difficult and again it was only another fine innings by Braund (50*), out of a meagre total of 120, that left Worcestershire a fairly easy task in scoring 160, which they did for the loss of only 2 wickets. Pearson had proved to be the best bowler on either side, again taking 4 wickets at a modest cost of 27 runs, which gave him match figures of 8 for 87 from 28 overs.

Jack White bowled more than 54 overs in the first innings and conceded only 66 runs with 4 wickets, but could not break through in the second innings in which he remained wicket-less.

Len Braund.

Frank Chester.

Somerset v. Worcestershire

PLAYED AT

WORCESTER, Thursday, Friday and Saturday, June 26th, 27th and 28th, 1913.

Lost by 8 wickets.

SOMERSET.

	First Innings.		Second Innings.	
Mr. M. P. Bajana	... b Burrows	... 7	c Pearson b Burns ...	32
Hyman	... c Burns b Pearson	41	b Burrows ...	6
Mr. R. E. Hancock	... c Bale b Burrows	2	b Burns ...	10
Braund	... not out	... 257	b Pearson ...	50
Mr. E. S. M. Poyntz	... c Bowley b Burrows	... 0	c Chester b Burns ...	1
Mr. H. Southwood	... c Bale b Burns	13	c Bale b Burns ...	0
Robson	.... c and b Burrows	12	b Pearson ...	1
Mr. C. G. Deane	... c Arnold b Pearson	23	b Pearson ...	0
Mr. B. D. Hylton-Stewart...	b Pearson	9	run out ...	13
Chidgey	... c Bale b Pearson	1	not out ...	0
Mr. J. C. White	... c Bale b Cuffe	11	b Pearson ...	0
	B 3, l-b 1, w 1, n-b 2	... 7	B 7 ...	7
	Total ...	383	Total ...	120

WORCESTERSHIRE.

	First Innings.		Second Innings.	
Bowley	... b White	... 25	c Chidgey b Hylton-Stewart	48
Pearson	... b White	... 11	not out ...	71
Mr. H. K. Foster	... c Chidgey b Hylton-Stewart	4	c Poyntz b Deane ...	27
Mr. W. B. Burns	..: b White	... 35	not out ...	5
Arnold	... b Robson	... 18		
Cuffe	... c Bajana b Hylton-Stewart	79		
Mr. G. H. Simpson-Hayward	b White	... 0		
Chester	... c Poyntz b Robson	... 115		
Hunt	... lbw b Robson	... 31		
Burrows	... not out	... 12		
Bale	... c Poyntz b Robson	... 4		
	B 4, l-b 4, w 2	... 10	B 8, l-b 1 ...	9
	Total ...	344	Total (for 2 wickets)	160

BOWLING ANALYSIS.

SOMERSET.		First Innings.				Second Innings.			
		O	M	R	W	O	M	R	W
Burrows	...	26	2	146	4	9	0	39	1
Mr. Burns	...	13	2	47	1	15	2	47	4
Hunt	...	4	0	19	0	—	—	—	—
Cuffe	...	13.3	1	48	1	—	—	—	—
Mr. Simpson-Hayward	...	7	2	27	0	—	—	—	—
Pearson	...	20	3	60	4	8	2	27	4
Chester	...	5	0	29	0	—	—	—	—

Chester bowled one wide, and Burrows two no-balls.

WORCESTERSHIRE.		First Innings.				Second Innings.			
Robson	...	35.1	3	140	4	7	2	32	0
Mr. Hylton-Stewart	...	22	2	68	2	9	1	38	1
Braund	...	8	1	44	0	—	—	—	—
Mr. White	...	54	25	66	4	17	5	37	0
Mr. Deane	...	3	0	16	0	4.5	0	21	1
Mr. Hancock	...	—	—	—	—	5	0	23	0

Mr. Deane bowled two wides.

Umpires—A. E. Street and W. Vining.

GLOUCESTERSHIRE

3, 4 August 1914 at Bristol

The imminent fear of war overshadowed the start of this game, although few realised that it would be over four years before a return game would be played. With everyone's minds on other things, the Rippon twins opened the innings for Somerset. Whilst both scrambled into double figures, only Len Braund (with 28*) faced the Gloucestershire bowlers with any confidence and Somerset were all out for 82.

Gloucestershire could do little better, thanks to some outstanding bowling by Jack White. An early run-out of opening batsman, Langdon, was all that prevented him from taking all 10 wickets, admittedly on a rain-damaged pitch. His final figures of 9 for 46 from 23.4 overs showed his remarkable skill and control of what must have been a wet ball for most of the innings. It was only a stand between Jessop and Roberts that prevented a complete rout, but a final total of 111 gave a 29-run advantage to the home side.

Somerset's second innings was almost a carbon copy of the first, with wickets falling with monotonous regularity. P.R. Johnson was the only batsman to establish himself and he scored an invaluable 40 runs in his customary stylish manner, though the other ten batsmen could muster only 65 runs between them and a final total of 105 left Gloucestershire just 77 runs to get for victory.

With 4 Gloucestershire wickets falling for only 10 runs, either side could have won this intriguing game, and when C.S. Barnett and Smith took the score to 74 for 7, it appeared to be all over for Somerset. However, panic set in and two wickets fell, both run out. Parker, walking to the crease, was far from happy with his colleagues for putting him in this awkward position but he survived, whilst Barnett hit the winning run, ending with 32*.

It was an exciting finish to a match which saw Jack White take 14 wickets yet end up on the losing side, whilst that other great left-arm bowler, Charlie Parker, could only manage 2 wickets for the winning side.

'Farmer' White.

SOMERSET.

Mr. A. D. E. Rippon b Jessop	19	— st Smith b Parker	0
Mr. A. E. S. Rippon c Parker b Dennett	15	— b Dennett	6
Mr. P. R. Johnson c Jessop b Dennett	6	— c Jessop b Dennett	40
Mr. B. L. Bisgood c Langdon b Dennett	0	— lbw, b Dennett	8
L. C. Braund not out	28	— c Dennett b Cranfield	6
Mr. E. S. M. Poyntz c Roberts b Jessop	2	— c Smith b Dennett	8
E. Robson c Smith b Dennett	4	— run out	0
Mr. P. P. Hope c Dipper b Dennett	0	— st Smith b Dennett	0
Mr. J. C. White lbw, b Dennett	5	— c Smith b Jessop	19
J. F. Bridges b Jessop	0	— not out	0
H Chidgey b Jessop	0	— c Sewell b Parker	13
L-b	3	B 2, l-b 2, n-b 1	5
	82		**105**

GLOUCESTERSHIRE.

T. Langdon run out	7	— c and b Robson	12
A. G. Dipper c Braund b White	5	— c and b White	3
Mr. C. O. H. Sewell b White	9	— c and b White	2
Mr. F. B. Roberts c Bridges b White	20	— c Bisgood b White	0
Mr. G. L. Jessop st Chidgey b White	25	— st Chidgey b White	4
Mr. C. S. Barnett c Bisgood b White	1	— not out	32
T. J. Smith b White	10	— b A. D. E. Rippon	13
L. Cranfield b White	0	— run out	0
Mr. M. A. Green c Braund b White	17	— run out	1
C. Parker c Robson b White	3	— not out	0
G. Dennett not out	4	— b White	5
B 8, l-b 1, n-b 1	10	B 4, l-b 1	5
	111		**77**

GLOUCESTERSHIRE BOWLING.

	Overs	Mdns.	Runs	Wkts.	Overs	Mdns.	Runs	Wkts.
Dennett	31	13	36	6	36	23	32	5
Cranfield	12	7	9	0	17	5	35	1
Jessop	19.5	5	34	4	7	4	7	1
Parker					12	5	26	2

SOMERSET BOWLING.

	Overs	Mdns.	Runs	Wkts.	Overs	Mdns.	Runs	Wkts.
White	23.4	8	46	9	18.1	6	32	5
Robson	15	3	38	0	9	1	26	1
A. D. E. Rippon	8	4	17	0	9	2	14	1

Umpires : A. E. Street and H. Butt.

Courtesy of Wisden Cricketers' Almanack.

YORKSHIRE

27, 28 August 1914 at Weston-Super-Mare

The First World War had begun and there was a strange feeling about cricket that was still scheduled to be played. It was agreed that the first ever Weston-Super-Mare festival should proceed, and Yorkshire were to provide the opposition.

It was a strange Yorkshire side without an amateur available, and George Hirst had the honour of leading his county. They were still the strongest club by far, and it was every other county's aim to beat them – even a draw was quite an achievement. With a newly-laid, untried pitch and a heavy atmosphere, their international bowlers, Booth, Rhodes, Hirst and Drake, were looking forward to an easy victory and time off to enjoy the sea air.

It was, however, Bridges and Braund, two stalwart Somerset bowlers, who were soon to be amongst the wickets when Yorkshire, on winning the toss, decided to bat. Had it not been for two solid innings by Denton and Drake, Yorkshire would have been in severe trouble, but a dropped catch helped the visitors to reach 162. This apparently low score was, however, thought by Hirst to be a winning total.

His thoughts were soon proved to be right, for Booth and Drake both took 5 wickets each and Somerset were all out in just one hour for a meagre 44, with Robson top-scoring with 19. Booth, with his fast right-arm deliveries, was a perfect foil for Drake's slower left-arm style and Somerset never looked like making an acceptable score.

Yorkshire fared badly in their second innings and were all out for 112, with 5 wickets to Robson and 4 to Bridges – Wilfred Rhodes top-scored with 25 and Somerset were left with 231 runs to get to win. With all the recognised batsmen back in the pavilion and with very few runs scored, it was left to two part-time amateurs, P.P. Hope and H.D. Harcombe, to add 37 for the 9th wicket, with Somerset finally totalling 90.

For Yorkshire there was even greater glory than an overwhelming victory. In Somerset's second innings, Alonzo Drake took all 10 wickets and became the first ever Yorkshire cricketer to accomplish this feat. Hirst and Rhodes, two of the best bowlers in the world, were not required in either innings and only 37.5 overs were needed to dismiss Somerset twice.

Neither Booth nor Drake were ever to play in Weston again, which no doubt pleased Somerset's batsmen, although they must have been greatly saddened by the news of Booth's death during the war and Drake's enforced retirement due to ill health.

Far left: *Alonzo Drake.*
Left: *Major Booth.*

YORKSHIRE.

M. W. Booth c Poyntz b Bridges......	1	— b Bridges 9
B. B. Wilson c Saunders b Bridges....	20	— b Bridges 9
D. Denton c Chidgey b Hylton-Stewart	52	— c Saunders b Bridges 0
R. Kilner c Hylton-Stewart b Bridges..	2	— c Braund b Bridges 4
W. Rhodes c and b Hylton-Stewart....	1	— lbw, b Robson 25
T. J. Birtles lbw, b Braund..........	16	— b Robson 10
A. Drake c Harcombe b Braund......	51	— c Hope b Robson 12
P. Holmes b Bridges................	7	— not out 3
G. H. Hirst c Bisgood b Bridges	5	— c Saunders b Robson 10
E. Oldroyd not out..................	0	— b Hylton-Stewart 23
A. Dolphin b Braund................	0	— b Robson 0
B 5, n-b 2....................	7	B 4, l-b 2, w 1.......... 7
	162	**112**

SOMERSET.

Mr. B. L. Bisgood c and b Booth........	6	— c Dolphin b Drake 11
L. C. Braund b Drake..............	1	— b Drake 9
E. Robson c Rhodes b Booth..........	19	— c Birtles b Drake 3
Mr. B. D. Hylton-Stewart b Drake....	1	— st Dolphin b Drake 3
W. Hyman b Drake..............	1	— st Dolphin b Drake 4
Mr. E. S. M. Poyntz b Drake..........	0	— c Oldroyd b Drake 5
Mr. P. P. Hope b Booth	3	— c and b Drake............ 19
Mr. H. W. Saunders b Drake..........	0	— b Drake 0
Mr. H. D. Harcombe not out..........	5	— b Drake 26
J. F. Bridges c Drake b Booth..........	7	— not out 1
H. Chidgey c Holmes b Booth........	0	— b Drake 4
B	1	B 4, n-b 1 5
	44	**90**

SOMERSET BOWLING.

	Overs	Mdns.	Runs	Wkts.	Overs	Mdns.	Runs	Wkts.
Robson........	14	5	45	0	14	2	38	5
Bridges........	17	1	59	5	14	1	54	4
Hylton-Stewart .	9	0	38	2	2	0	6	1
Braund........	8.4	2	13	3	4	2	7	0

YORKSHIRE BOWLING.

	Overs	Mdns.	Runs	Wkts.	Overs	Mdns.	Runs	Wkts.
Booth	8	0	27	5	9	0	50	0
Drake	7	1	16	5	8.5	0	35	10

Umpires : A. E. Street and A. Millward.

Courtesy of Wisden Cricketers' Almanack.

SUSSEX

21, 22 May 1919 at Taunton

With the First World War over, but not forgotten, cricket restarted and Somerset were still relying largely on amateurs. In fact, they fielded seven in all in this match, which included only three players from the last match in 1914.

The Rippon twins opened the innings with Dudley being the more forceful in scoring a valuable 60. With the help of P.P. Hope, better known as the captain of Bath Rugby Club, Somerset had to be satisfied with a first-innings total of 243. George Cox had caused a lot of trouble with his slow left-arm deliveries and had achieved the fine figures of 5 for 51.

Sussex, always an attractive batting side, lost a quick wicket. Bridges and Robson continued to make life difficult for them, but the appearance of Maurice Tate, recognised more as a batsman than as a bowler at this stage of his career, with help from Cox saw Sussex reach 242. Mr H.T. Heygate, a useful amateur batsman, whose 'muscular pains' prevented him from taking his normal place in the batting order came in at number eleven, but was unable to trouble the score.

Second time around, Somerset lost 3 quick wickets to George Cox and were considered fortunate to total 103 with Bridges top-scoring with just 14. A Sussex victory seemed certain, but Somerset had an inspired day in the field, with Bridges and Braund outstanding. Sussex were reduced to 48 for 6 although the opening batsman, Mr H.L. Wilson, appeared to be unmoveable. With the score on 103, an 'inspired' bowling change saw a very occasional bowler, Dudley Rippon, take the ball and he soon had 2 wickets to his credit at a cost of a single run. The scores were level when Bridges caught Miller off the bowling of White and it was at this time that the real excitement broke out.

Mr Heygate, who had not fielded, was still struggling with various aches and pains when he was asked if he would bat. Agreeing, he attempted to reach the crease, dressed in ordinary clothes plus pads strapped on by fellow players, but by this time the umpires had declared the match to be over and he was 'timed out' under Law 45. This decision was criticised by many, but the umpire's decision was upheld and it remains the only example of such a dismissal in first-class cricket.

So ended Heygate's career of just six matches for Sussex, covering 1903-1919, although he had also played for Canada against the USA in 1908.

Maurice Tate.

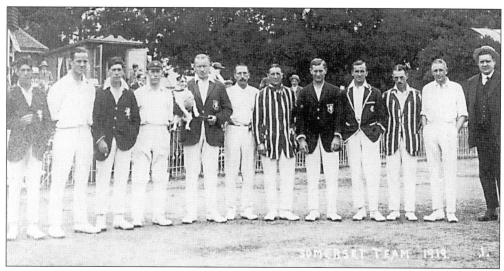

Somerset CCC, 1919. From left to right: S. Rippon, J. Bridges, H. Chidgey, E.S.M. Pontz, E. Robson, J. daniel, J.C. White, N. Hardy, J.C.W. McBryan, S. McAulay (scorer).

G. Cox (Senior).

H.L. Wilson.

Somerset v. Sussex (continued).

UMPIRES			SCORERS		

SIDE WINNING TOSS FOR CHOICE OF INNINGS.

MATCH PLAYED AT *Somerset* ON 19

Second INNINGS

ORDER	BATSMEN'S NAMES	RUNS AS SCORED	HOW OUT	BOWLER	TOTALS	
1	A.D.E. Rippon	621 —	c Roberts	Cox	8	1.
2	A.E.S. Rippon	3IIII ✓	Bowled	Cox	8	4
3	J.C.W. MacBryan	I	Bowled	Cox	0	2
4	Robson C	21IIII21 ✓	Bowled	Roberts	11	2
5	Braund Lt	3III4 ✓	Bowled	Roberts	11	5
7b	Bridges J. Amer.	III1213II13 ✓	st Miller	Vincett	14	7
6.	Capt. Amor.	I4III3 ✓	c Cox	Tate	13	6
8	P.P. Hope	II2 ✓	Stannard	Vincett	6	8
9	J.D. Harcombe	212 ✓	Run	Out	5	9
10	J.C. White	I22321	Not	Out	11	
11	Chidgey H.	II322	c Vincett	Cox	10	10
BYES II		LEG BYES	WIDES I	NO BALLS	TOTAL EXTRAS	6
					TOTAL	103.

RUNS AT THE FALL OF EACH WICKET	1 FOR 11.	2 FOR 13.	3 FOR 22.	4 FOR 32.	5 FOR 44.	6 FOR 71.	7 FOR 71.	8 FOR 82.	9 FOR 85.	10 FOR 103

COPYRIGHT REGISTERED.

Scorebook – Somerset's second innings.

J.C. White.

SOMERSET v. SUSSEX.

Played at TAUNTON, Wednesday, Thursday, May 21, 22. — 1919

SOMERSET.

Mr. A. E. S. Rippon c Miller b Stannard	26	—	b Cox	8
Mr. A. D. E. Rippon c Miller b Vincett..	60	—	b Cox	8
Mr. J. C. W. McBryan lbw, b Cox....	18	—	b Cox	0
E. Robson b Cox	14	—	b Roberts	11
L. C. Braund b Roberts	3	—	b Roberts	11
Mr. J. D. Harcombe c H. Wilson b Cox	0	—	run out	5
Mr. P. P. Hope c Tate b Vincett	48	—	c Stannard b Vincett	6
J. F. Bridges c Miller b Vincett	34	—	st Miller b Vincett	14
Capt. Amor b Cox	14	—	c Cox b Tate	13
Mr. J. C. White b Cox	12	—	not out	11
H. Chidgey not out	1	—	c Vincett b Cox	10
B 8, lb 4, w 1	13		B 5, w 1	6
	243			**103**

SUSSEX.

Mr. H. L. Wilson b Bridges	56	—	not out	42
Mr. A. K. Wilson c Braund, b Bridges	4	—	c Braund b Robson	4
Mr. T. E. Bourdillon b Bridges	21	—	c Bridges b Robson	7
Mr. A. C. Somerset b Robson	33	—	c Braund b Robson	0
Mr. R. A. T. Miller b Bridges	2	—	c Bridges b White	0
Mr. J. H. Vincett b Bridges	14	—	b Bridges	6
H. E. Roberts b Robson	5	—	b D. Rippon	28
M. W. Tate c Braund b Robson	69	—	c Chidgey b Bridges	11
G. Stannard b A. D. E. Rippon	3	—	c McBryan b D. Rippon	0
G. Cox not out	24	—	b Bridges	0
Mr. H. J. Heygate b White	0	—	absent	0
B 5, lb 6	11		B 1, l-b 5	6
	242			**104**

SUSSEX BOWLING.

	Overs	Mdns.	Runs	Wkts.	Overs	Mdns.	Runs	Wkts.
Roberts	17	4	51	1	16	1	40	2
Vincett	31	4	69	3	9	0	20	2
Stannard	8	0	27					
Tate	12	3	32	0	6	1	11	1
Cox	15.4	4	51	5	18.4	6	26	4

SOMERSET BOWLING.

	Overs	Mdns.	Runs	Wkts.	Overs	Mdns.	Runs	Wkts.
White	18.4	1	76	1	33	0	14	1
Robson	15	3	49	3	14	2	51	3
Bridges	22	4	84	5	12	2	32	3
D. Rippon	9	2	22	1	2	1	1	2

Umpires : F. G. Roberts and A. E. Street.

Courtesy of Wisden Cricketers' Almanack.

GLOUCESTERSHIRE

2, 3 August 1920 at Bristol

Odd things can happen in cricket, but in this holiday fixture the result was almost unbelievable. John Daniell underestimated the quality of the Gloucestershire batsmen when he declared his side's second innings closed.

Somerset, batting first, got off to a dreadful start with A.E.S. Rippon run out after scoring a single and in a side that contained ten amateurs plus Robson they continued to struggle. A top score of 45 by F.A. Waldock helped them to an inadequate 169 before it was Gloucestershire's turn to bat. Parker and Dennett had each taken 4 wickets and on a wicket that was giving help to the slow bowlers. Somerset were looking forward to the challenge. Their success was much greater than anyone could have imagined.

Robson and White opened the bowling to C.L. Townsend and Dipper who were to put together the highest stand of an innings that was over, almost before it had started, for just 22 runs. The highest individual score was 5 each by Dipper and Wilson. White proved to be almost unplayable and ended with the astonishing figures of 7 for 10 from 9 overs (4 of them maidens) whilst Robson had 3 for 12, again from 9 overs, 4 of which were maidens.

With a lead of 147, Somerset thought that victory was for the taking and some reckless batting followed until, with the score on 126 for 7, Daniell decided that he had enough runs on the board to declare and leave Gloucestershire to chase 274 to win. It was a decision that backfired. A brilliant innings by C.L. Townsend, scoring 84 out of 119 in around 70 minutes, solid support from Dipper (48) and sensible batting by the middle order saw Gloucestershire bring off one of their greatest ever victories.

Though White and Robson tried hard, they could not repeat their first innings form and took only 3 wickets between them, leaving Daniell to regret his decision to declare as Gloucestershire eased to a 4-wicket victory.

C.L. Townsend.

J. Daniell.

Somerset v. Gloucestershire.

PLAYED AT

BRISTOL, SATURDAY, MONDAY, TUESDAY, July 31, August 2, 3, 1920.

Somerset lost by 4 wickets.

SOMERSET.

	First Innings.		Second Innings	
Mr. A. E. S. Rippon	run out	1		
Mr. J. A. S. Jackson	c Williams b Parker	5	b Parker	10
Mr. J. C. W. MacBryan	b Parker	38	not out	29
Mr. M. D. Lyon	c Mills b Dennett	12	lbw b Parker	41
Mr. F. A. Waldock	c Williams b Parker	45	run out	2
Mr. M. L. Hambling	c P. G. Robinson b Dennett	3	b Parker	1
Mr. J. Daniell	c Williams b Parker	34	c F. G. Robinson b Mills	24
Mr. P. A. Foy	c and b Dipper	8	b Mills	2
Robson	c Rowlands b Dennett	4		
Mr. J. C. White	c F. G. Robinson b Dennett	8	b Mills	10
Mr. J. J. Bridges	not out	0		
	B 7, l-b 3, n-b 1	11	B 5, l-b 2	7

Total 169   Total (for 7 wickets) *126

*Innings declared closed.

GLOUCESTERSHIRE.

	First Innings.		Second Innings.	
Mr. C. L. Townsend	lbw b Robson	4	c Robson b Bridges	84
Dipper	c Daniell b White	5	b Bridges	48
Mr. W. H. Rowlands	b Robson	0	c MacBryan b White	7
Smith	c Daniell b White	1	c White b Robson	1
Mr. P. G. Robinson	c and b White	2	c Waldock b Robson	37
Mr. M. A. Green	c MacBryan b White	3	not out	32
Mr. F. G. Robinson	c Daniell b White	0	b Bridges	28
Mr. P. F. C. Williams	b Robson	5	not out	14
Mills	st Lyon b White	0		
Parker	c and b White	2		
Dennett	not out	0		
			B 18, l-b 7	25

Total 22   Total (for 6 wickets) 276

BOWLING ANALYSIS.

SOMERSET.	First Innings.					Second Innings.			
	O.	M.	R.	W.		O.	M.	R.	W.
Dennett	38.5	16	68	4		15	4	43	0
Parker	39	20	58	4		19	5	41	3
Dipper	7	2	19	1		—	—	—	—
Mills	6	2	13	0		13.3	2	35	3

Parker bowled one no-ball.

GLOUCESTERSHIRE.	First Innings.					Second Innings.			
Robson	9	4	12	3		23	3	68	2
Mr. J. C. White	9	4	10	7		25	7	65	1
Mr. J. J. Bridges	—	—	—	—		20	4	74	3
Mr. P. A. Foy	—	—	—	—		4	0	24	0
Mr. M. L. Hambling	—	—	—	—		8	3	20	0

Umpires: A. E. Street and J. Blake.

WORCESTERSHIRE

18, 20, 21 June 1920 at Worcester

Although Somerset finally won by 83 runs, it had been a close and interesting game of cricket over three days, with the final wicket falling with only 15 minutes of play remaining.

Somerset batted first and were indebted to Robson who scored 111 out of a modest total of 237 on a good wicket. Fielding a side that was far from full strength – they had four amateurs who were to play little first-class cricket and had to include two wicketkeepers, Spurway and Chidgley, in making up a makeshift XI – it was a reasonable first innings total.

Worcestershire fought hard, but there was to be only one hero, Jack White. Bowling 42 overs and 2 balls, he took all 10 wickets at a cost of only 76 runs, keeping a stranglehold on all the batsmen. Robson and Hunt shared the bowling at the other end, each striving for wickets, but White calmly worked his way through the order. Riley, M.F.S. Jewell and Pearson were the only Worcestershire batsmen to play him with any confidence but even so they managed to equal Somerset's first-innings total.

Batting a second time another hero arrived, this time a batsman in the shape of P.R. Johnson. Opening the innings with John Daniell, they saw 154 runs on the scoreboard before Daniell was out for 38. Johnson completely dominated the innings with a magnificent 163, but Tarbox, who had not bowled in the first innings, achieved fine figures of 7 for 55 restricting the final score to 364.

Needing 365 runs to win in 285 minutes was always going to be a difficult task, but Worcestershire set about it with confidence, and an attractive opening partnership, plus a rapid 24 from Turner, saw them reach 210 for the loss of only 3 wickets. Bowley was within a run of a well-deserved century when he was bowled by Robson, Pearson fell for a gallant 80 and when 2 further wickets fell to Robson, the game had turned in Somerset's favour. White then got amongst the remaining wickets and Worcestershire's brave attempt to score 365 came to an end when they were finally dismissed for 281 – some 83 runs short of their target.

Robson took 5 for 85 and White 5 for 99, giving him match figures of 15 for 175. This fell short of his best ever 16 for 83, which was achieved against Worcestershire at Bath in 1919.

J.C. White.

F.L. Bowley.

Somerset v. Worcestershire

PLAYED AT

WORCESTER, SATURDAY, MONDAY, and TUESDAY, June 18, 20, 21; 1921.

Somerset won by 83 runs.

SOMERSET.

	First Innings.		Second Innings.	
Mr. P. R. Johnson	c Ponsonby b Richardson	4	b Tarbox	..163
Mr. J. Daniell	c Ponsonby b Humpherson	24	lbw, b Richardson	.. 38
Mr. F. E. Spurway	c Higgins b Richardson	.. 0	c Turner b Tarbox	.. 31
Mr. T. C. Lowry	b Humpherson	.. 22	b Richardson	.. 18
Mr. L. E. Wharton	lbw, b Gilbert	.. 38	c Ponsonby b Tarbox	.. 36
Robson (E.)	c Tarbox b Pearson	..111	b Tarbox	.. 8
Mr. P. P. Hope	b Gilbert	.. 13	b Tarbox	.. 8
Mr. J. C. White	b Gilbert	.. 6	b Tarbox	.. 29
Mr. L. H. Key	b Pearson	.. 5	c Bowley b Richardson	.. 3
Hunt (G.)	b Pearson	.. 3	b Tarbox	.. 10
Chidgey (H.)	not out	.. 6	not out	.. 0
	B 3, l-b 2	.. 5	B 14, l-b 3, w 1, n-b 2	20
	Total ..237		Total ..364	

WORCESTERSHIRE.

	First Innings.		Second Innings.	
Bowley	c Lowry b White	.. 1	b Robson	.. 99
Pearson (F.)	c and b White	.. 74	b Robson	.. 80
Turner (R. E.)	b White	.. 12	b Robson	.. 24
Mr. H. L. Higgins	lbw, b White	.. 16	b Robson	.. 3
Mr. M. F. S. Jewell	st Chidgey b White	.. 66	lbw, b White	.. 2
Mr. W. E. Richardson	b White	.. 7	c Daniell b White	.. 0
Preece (C. A.)	c Daniell b White	.. 27	b White	.. 0
Tarbox (C. V.)	b White	.. 13	c Spurway b White	.. 17
Mr. C. H. B. Ponsonby	lbw, b White	.. 0	c Lowry b White	.. 15
Mr. V. W. Humpherson	not out	.. 2	b Robson	.. 13
Mr. H. A. Gilbert	c Hope b White	.. 0	not out	.. 0
	B 14, l-b 5	.. 19	B 20, l-b 7, w 1	.. 28
	Total ..237		Total ..281	

Bowling Analysis.

SOMERSET.	First Innings.					Second Innings.			
	O.	M.	R.	W.		O.	M.	R.	W.
Mr. Gilbert	32	6	99	3		28	2	100	0
Mr. Richardson	18	4	60	2		16	3	59	3
Mr. Humpherson	9	1	36	2		9	2	38	0
Pearson	10.4	3	32	3		12	0	48	0
Preece	2	0	5	0		6	0	36	0
Mr. Jewell	—	—	—	—		4	0	8	0
Tarbox	—	—	—	—		14.5	3	55	7

Mr. Richardson bowled 1 wide and 2 no-balls.

WORCESTERSHIRE.	First Innings.					Second Innings.			
Robson	25	4	71	0		39.5	15	83	5
Mr. White	42.2	11	76	10		47	19	99	5
Hunt	18	4	55	0		15	4	42	0
Mr. Wharton	6	2	16	0		9	1	29	0

Robson bowled 1 wide.

Umpires : J. Carlin and J. Moss.

GLOUCESTERSHIRE

30 July, 1, 2 August 1921 at Bristol

What appeared at first sight to be an ordinary County match, came to life on the final afternoon with Gloucestershire winning by one wicket. Somerset batted first and had P.R. Johnson in their side – he had made his debut way back in 1901 – but his first innings contribution was negligible. No batsmen was ever able to dominate the bowling and MacBryan was top scorer with 46 out of a total of 212. The highlight of the innings was the bowling of Parker, who well deserved all 10 wickets. It was a mammoth effort, opening the bowling and continuing throughout – 40.3 overs from which he conceded only 79 runs.

Gloucestershire lost an early wicket, but Seabrook and E.P. Barnett saw them past the 100-mark and the latter was unfortunate to miss his century by only 5 runs. A total of 248 gave them a lead of 36. All the Somerset bowlers had some success, but Jack White was once again the 'star', taking 3 for 51 from 44 overs (which included 25 maidens).

No Somerset batsman was able to reach 50 when they batted a second time, although there were three scores in the 40s – MacBryan with 49, Tom Lowry 46 and John Daniell with 48 – which helped them to attain 240.

A target of 205 on a rain-affected pitch was never going to be easy and when wickets began to fall it appeared that Somerset were the more likely winners. A fine partnership by Smith and Robinson added 74 vital runs and for a time Gloucestershire were favourites. Smith with 60* batted for 125 minutes without giving a chance and whilst the run-out of Parker gave Somerset some hope, Dennett stayed with Smith until the target was reached.

Gloucestershire's extra-time victory, by a single wicket, when defeat had appeared to be a certainty, coupled with Parker's 10-wicket haul, resulted in long and noisy celebrations at the County Ground.

C.W.L. Parker.

Somerset v. Gloucestershire

PLAYED AT

BRISTOL, SATURDAY, MONDAY, and TUESDAY, JULY 30, AUGUST 1 and 2, 1921.

Somerset lost by 1 wicket.

SOMERSET.

	First Innings.		Second Innings.	
Mr. P. R. Johnson ..	c Barnett b Parker	.. 1	b Mills	.. 29
Mr. J. C. W. MacBryan .	c Williams b Parker	.. 46	st Robinson b Dennett	.. 49
Mr. T. C. Lowry ..	c Smith b Parker	.. 20	lbw, b Mills	.. 46
Young (A.) ..	b Parker	.. 34	b Mills	.. 28
Mr S. G. U. Considine ..	lbw, b Parker	. 23	b Parker	.. 8
Mr. L. E. Wharton ..	b Parker	.. 12	b Mills	.. 5
Mr. J. Daniell ..	st Robinson b Parker	.. 4	b Dennett	.. 48
Robson (E.) ..	c Smith b Parker	.. 7	c Mills b Parker	.. 5
Mr. J. C. White ..	lbw, b Parker	.. 16	c Mills b Parker	.. 0
Mr. J. J. Bridges ..	c Barnett b Parker	.. 24	c Rowlands b Mills	.. 5
Mr. R. C. Robertson-Glasgow ..	not out	.. 21	not out	.. 1
	L-b 3, w 1	.. 4	B 12, l-b 4	.. 16
	Total	..212	Total	..240

GLOUCESTERSHIRE.

	First Innings.		Second Innings.	
Dipper (A. G.) ..	lbw, b White	.. 53	c and b R.-Glasgow	.. 17
Mr. F. J. Seabrook ..	b Bridges	.. 6	lbw, b Robson	.. 11
Mr. E. P. Barnett ..	c Young b R.-Glasgow	.. 95	b Robson	.. 11
Mr. W. H. Rowlands ..	lbw, b White	.. 0	b Bridges	.. 0
Mr. P. F. C Williams ..	b Bridges	.. 14	c White b Robson	.. 15
Smith (H.) ..	c Lowry b Robson	.. 9	not out	.. 62
Mr. F. G. Robinson ..	b Robson	.. 10	b Young	.. 41
Mr. J. L. Stanton ..	c Young b White	.. 5	c Bridges b White	.. 8
Mills (P.) ..	c Bridges b R.-Glasgow ..	28	b Bridges	.. 24
Parker (C.) . ..	c Johnson b Bridges	.. 10	run out	.. 0
Dennett (G.) ..	not out	.. 6	not out	.. 0
	B 6, l-b 6	.. 12	B 5, l-b 9, w 2	.. 16
	Total	..248	Total (for 9 wkts.)	205

Bowling Analysis.

SOMERSET.	First Innings.					Second Innings.			
	O.	M.	R.	W.	..	O.	M.	R.	W.
Parker	.. 40.3	13	79	10	..	22	2	78	3
Mills	.. 38	7	116	0	..	26.3	2	92	5
Dennett	.. 2	0	13	0	..	21	7	42	2
Dipper	..				..	6	0	12	0

Dennett bowled 1 wide.

GLOUCESTERSHIRE.	First Innings.					Second Innings.			
Robson	.. 23	4	58	2	..	35	14	52	3
Mr. Bridges	.. 35.4	9	76	3	..	21.1	8	42	2
Mr. White	.. 44	25	51	3	..	28	8	56	1
Mr. Robertson-Glasgow	.. 19	5	38	2	..	8	3	26	1
Young	.. 4	0	13	0	..	7	2	13	1

Robson bowled 2 wides.

Umpires : J. Blake and H. Young.

SURREY

15, 17, 18 August 1925 at Taunton

This is probably the most reported match of the early part of the twentieth century and has forever been known as 'Jack Hobbs' match', even though it was played in Taunton. It was, of course, the match in which he first equalled and then beat the long-standing record of centuries held by W.G. Grace. He had started the season in great form, but after scoring his 125th century, nothing appeared to go right for him. He made good scores, but they failed to reach the magical 100 and rain had often prevented play, so he was looking forward to playing on Taunton's good wicket and exploiting its short boundaries.

There was a very large crowd to greet the 'master', but they had to wait to see him bat as Somerset had won the toss and elected to bat. Patience was rewarded when Somerset were bowled out for 167, with only Young scoring a half-century. Lockton took 4 wickets off 16 overs for only 36 runs, but the moment that everyone was waiting for was fast approaching.

With his usual partner, Andy Sandham, Hobbs strolled to the crease at the beginning of an innings that would enter the record books. With 140 minutes left to play, the spectators were hoping to see Grace's record equalled, but it was not to be. Indeed, they were fortunate to see any of Hobbs' magic as he was caught out in the first over from what was, luckily for him, called a no-ball.

He batted with extreme caution, particularly when facing Jack White, and after the tea interval he was able to increase his rate of scoring, although he still required 53 in the remaining 45 minutes. However, when he had scored 86, he was called for a quick single by his batting partner, D.J. Knight. It was thanks to Knight, who sacrificed his own wicket, that Hobbs was able to continue his innings. However, when stumps were drawn at the end on Saturday's play he still required 9 more runs to reach that ilusive century.

Another very large crowd awaited the players on the Monday morning and they did not have long to wait before the celebrations were underway. A no-ball was struck to the boundary and, together with 4 singles, his score reached 99*. Finally squeezing a ball from Bridges to square leg, he recorded his 126th century and the celebrations could begin.

The Surrey captain brought champagne to the wicket and all the players and spectators entered into the celebrations. Indeed, the game was held up for some time. When play resumed, he was soon caught at the wicket by M.L. Hall off the bowling of Bridges for 101 and the Surrey innings closed on 359, a lead of 192.

J.M.C. MacBryan was not to be overshadowed and with Young threatened to take the game away from Surrey. He scored a superb 109 out in around 130 minutes with 16 boundaries. These runs were scored out of only 184 and at the close of play on the second day, Somerset had a lead of 64 with 7 wickets still standing.

Late runs by Hunt and Bridges saw 374 saw the total reach 374, leaving Surrey needing 183 to win this fascinating match. All efforts by the Somerset bowlers failed to break the opening partnership, and Hobbs finally delighted even the Somerset players by scoring his second century of the match, thus beating the record set by W.G. Grace. Sandham played a most unselfish innings, manipulating the strike to allow Hobbs as much of the bowling as possible and ended up with 74*.

Not only did Hobbs break the longstanding record of W.G. Grace, but his second hundred was his 14th of the season, which created yet another record for this great batsman. He went on to record two further centuries before the season was over, scoring in all 16 in his 3,024 runs at an average of 70.32.

The record-breaking run.

Jack Hobbs celebrates his great achievement.

Jack Hobbs.

Andy Sandham.

E.R.T. Holmes.

H. Strudwick.

SOMERSET *v* SURREY

Played at the County Ground, Taunton, 15, 17 and 18 August 1925

SURREY WON BY 10 WICKETS

SOMERSET	FIRST INNINGS		SECOND INNINGS	
J. C. W. MacBryan	b Holmes	6	b Fender	109
A. Young	c Sadler b Lockton	58	c Strudwick b Sadler	71
T. E. S. Francis	b Sadler	0	c Strudwick b Lockton	12
*J. C. White	b Sadler	1	c Strudwick b Sadler	30
P. R. Johnson	c and b Lockton	30	c Peach b Fender	16
E. F. Longrigg	b Sadler	5	run out	4
R. A. Ingle	b Fender	22	c Shepherd b Peach	23
G. Hunt	b Lockton	4	b Fender	59
R. C. Robertson-Glasgow	c Jardine b Lockton	4	c Sadler b Fender	5
J. J. Bridges	c and b Shepherd	25	b Fender	26
†M. L. Hill	not out	0	not out	1
Extras	lb 8, w 4	12	b 9, lb 5, nb 4	18
Total		167		374

BOWLING	O	M	R	W	O	M	R	W
Sadler	16	4	28	3	21	2	59	2
Holmes	6	2	12	1	17	0	56	0
Fender	13	3	39	1	35.5	8	120	5
Lockton	16	4	36	4	9	2	15	1
Peach	9	2	21	0	20	7	46	1
Shepherd	6.3	1	19	1	21	5	60	0

SURREY	FIRST INNINGS		SECOND INNINGS	
Hobbs, J. B.	c Hill b Bridges	101	not out	101
A. Sandham	c Longrigg b Bridges	13	not out	74
D. J. Knight	run out	34		
T. F. Shepherd	b White	0		
D. R. Jardine	run out	47		
E. R. T. Holmes	c Hill b Robertson-Glasgow	24		
*P. G. H. Fender	st Hill b Young	59		
H. A. Peach	b Young	20		
W. C. H. Sadler	c Johnson b Young	25		
†H. Strudwick	not out	10		
J. H. Lockton	absent	—		
Extras	b 15, lb 8, nb 3	26	b 6, lb 1, nb 1	8
Total		359	(for no wkt)	183

BOWLING	O	M	R	W	O	M	R	W
Robertson-Glasgow	26	1	144	1	6	0	42	0
Bridges	37	5	115	2	11	3	27	0
White	29	13	51	1	14	6	34	0
Hunt	4	1	14	0	8	4	15	0
Young	5.3	1	9	3	15.5	1	39	0
Longrigg					3	0	18	0

Umpires: H. Draper and H. Young

ESSEX

17, 18, 19 June 1926 at Chelmsford

A match in which the excitement continued long after the game was over with the result finally clarified after being referred to the MCC. It was the first match on the new Chelmsford ground and the bowlers had the upper hand from the start. Nicholls and Russell each took 3 wickets for Essex and restrained all the Somerset batsmen with the exception of MacBryan, who scored an impressive 80 – although it took him almost 3 hours to do so.

Somerset had nine amateurs in their side but for once every one was worthy of a place and all made a useful contribution even though their final total was only 208.

Essex also struggled against good bowling by White and Hunt – they bowled almost 75 per cent of the overs that were required to dismiss Essex for 178 – giving Somerset a first-innings lead of 30.

Batting became even more difficult when Somerset batted a second time, and they were considered lucky to reach 107 by the time the final wicket fell. A typically stubborn 23* from Case and a few hefty blows from J.J. Bridges (17) saved them from a total collapse.

Requiring 138 runs to win, Essex started well with Freeman and Cutmore posting 50 but the White-Bridges combination coupled with more and more help from the wicket ran through the middle order; when Essex were 8 wickets down Eastman, in attempting to win the match, was caught by Earle off the bowling of Bridges.

It was at this stage that the confusion began. There was less than a minute of playing time remaining and the umpires deemed the match to be over. The scores were level, but under the rules prevailing at the time Somerset were entitled to the points as a result of their first-innings lead. John Daniell wanted to continue but P. Perrin, the Essex captain, who was still not out, accepted the umpires' ruling. It was agreed to refer the matter to the MCC Rules committee, who finally declared the match to be a tie with the full match points being equally divided between the two Counties.

This was a rare case of a result being changed long after the match was over.

J.C.W. MacBryan.

M.D. Lyon.

A.C. Russell.

J. Cutmore.

J.J. Brides.

M.S. Nichols.

P.A. Perrin.

Somerset _v_, Essex.

PLAYED AT
CHELMSFORD, WEDNESDAY, THURSDAY and FRIDAY, JUNE 16, 17 and 18, 1926.

Tie.

SOMERSET.

First Innings.		Second Innings.	
J. Daniell b Nichols	21	b Nichols	2
Young c and b Russell	12	b Nichols ..	15
M. D. Lyon lbw b Russell	15	b Eastman ..	11
J. C. W. MacBryan c Perrin b Russell ..	80	b Eastman ..	12
J. C. White c Ridley b O'Connor ..	18	c and b Eastman ..	0
P. R. Johnson c O'Connor b H. M. Morris	24	b Nichols ..	0
C. C. Case run out	4	not out ..	23
G. F. Earle c Morris b Nichols ..	4	b Nichols ..	15
Hunt run out	0	b Eastman ...	9
M. L. Hill b Nichols	9	b Eastman ..	0
J. J. Bridges not out	1	c Nicholas b Eastman ..	17
Extras ..	20	Extras ..	3
Total	208	Total	107

ESSEX.

First Innings.		Second Innings.	
Freeman b Earle	43	c Hunt b Bridges ..	37
Cutmore c Hill b White	13	lbw b White ..	26
O'Connor c White b Hunt	10	c and b White ..	13
Russell c Lyon b White	10	b Hunt ..	4
Nichols c Johnson b Earle	0	b Bridges ..	23
Capt. F. W. Nicholas c Daniell b White	9	b Bridges ..	13
P. Perrin not out	19	not out ..	15
H. M. Morris b Hunt ..	12	b Hunt ..	0
G. N. N. Ridley c White b Hunt ..	4		
L. C. Eastman st Hill b White ..	0	c Earle b Bridges ..	0
Sir G. Rowley c Johnson b White ..	23	b Bridges ..	0
Extras ..	35	Extras ..	6
Total	178	Total (for 9 wkts.)	137

Bowling Analysis.

	First Innings.					Second Innings.			
SOMERSET	O.	M.	R.	W.		O.	M.	R.	W.
Nichols ..	21.5	3	48	3	..	15	2	45	4
L. C. Eastman	26	9	50	0	..	15	4	59	6
Sir G. Rowley	8	0	26	0	..	—	—	—	—
Russell ..	30	13	39	3	..	—	—	—	—
O'Connor ..	8	1	19	1	..	—	—	—	—
H. M. Morris ..	3	1	6	1	..	—	—	—	—
ESSEX ..	O.	M.	R.	W.		O.	M.	R.	W.
J. J. Bridges ..	15	6	24	0	..	16	4	33	5
G. F. Earle ..	7	2	10	2	..	3	1	13	0
J. C. White ..	44	21	57	5	..	22	5	49	2
Hunt	30	15	42	3	..	17	6	36	2
Young	6	2	10	0	..	—	—	—	—

Umpires : F. Chester and J. Stone.

ESSEX

7, 8, 9 August 1929 at Weston-Super-Mare

Overnight rain prevented any play before tea on the first day of this festival match, but Wellard was soon to make up for any time lost. In the final season with help from Jack White, 9 Essex wickets fell for just 100 runs with Eastman top scoring with a fortunate 30.

On the following morning it did not take Somerset long to collect the final wicket and White ended up taking 6 for 36 and Wellard 4 for 41. It was never going to be easy for Somerset to score runs and when Young and Longrigg had given them a good start of 82, wickets began to fall. Hipkin and O'Connor were responsible for a collapse from 82 for 1 to 132 all out – a lead of 26.

It was almost a repeat of the first innings when Essex batted for the second time. L.G. Crawley opened the innings and was their topscorer with just 23 to his name. White was once again responsible for their dismissal for 103 – his 6 for 31 from 27 overs was ably assisted by Jack Lee, who took 3 for 19 from 22.4 overs.

Could Somerset score 78 to win on a wicket that was giving considerable help to the slow bowlers? A second-wicket stand between Longrigg and Considine gave hope, but O'Connor and Hipkin had other ideas. They proved to be the equal of Somerset's slow bowlers, White and Lee, and when the Lee brothers failed with the bat, Essex became the favourites to win. For once Wellard failed to lay bat on ball and Essex ran out winners by 2 runs.

O'Connor had match figures of 8 for 47 and Hipkin 9 for 52 and whilst the holiday crowd had missed out on runs – only 408 were scored in four completed innings – they certainly saw some of the best slow bowling from both sides.

J. O'Connor.

Somerset *v.* Essex.

PLAYED AT

WESTON-SUPER-MARE, WEDNESDAY, THURSDAY and FRIDAY, AUGUST 7, 8
and 9, 1929.

Somerset lost by two runs.

ESSEX.

First Innings.		Second Innings.	
L. G. Crawley c Luckes b Wellard	9	c Young b White	23
Cutmore c & b Wellard	6	c Considine b Wellard	5
O'Connor c Longrigg b White	24	c Lee (J.W.) b White	4
Nicholls b Wellard	6	b Lee (J.)	21
Eastman (L.) c White b Wellard	30	lbw b White	7
H. M. Morris c Considine b White	0	c Longrigg b White	0
H. W. F. Franklin b White	11	c Ingle b White	5
Hipkin b White	6	c Wellard b White	10
F. W. Gilligan not out	4	b Lee (J.W.)	4
Wade b White	0	st Luckes b Lee (J.W.)	15
Sheffield c Wellard b White	2	not out	7
Extras	8	Extras	2
Total	**106**	**Total**	**103**

SOMERSET.

First Innings.		Second Innings.	
Young st Gilligan b Hipkin	33	c Wade b O'Connor	6
E. F. Longrigg c Hipkin b Nichols	48	c Gilligan b Hipkin	17
S. G. U. Considine b Nichols	1	b O'Connor	12
J. C. W. MacBryan b Hipkin	3	b Hipkin	1
J. C. White lbw b O'Connor	11	lbw b O'Connor	5
C. C. Case lbw b Hipkin	14	c Nichols b Hipkin	5
R. A. Ingle b O'Connor	2	not out	6
Lee (F.S.) not out	8	b Hipkin	10
Lee (J.W.) lbw b Hipkin	0	run out	1
Wellard b Hipkin	0	b O'Connor	4
Luckes b O'Connor	1	b O'Connor	2
Extras	11	Extras	6
Total	**132**	**Total**	**75**

Bowling Analysis.

ESSEX	First Innings.					Second Innings.			
	O.	M.	R.	W.		O.	M.	R.	W.
Wellard	19	6	41	4		22	10	49	1
J. C. White	27.2	13	36	6		27	15	31	6
Lee (J.W.)	8	3	21	0		22.4	15	19	3
Young						11	10	2	0

SOMERSET	O.	M.	R.	W.		O.	M.	R.	W.
Nichols	12	1	49	2		5	1	8	0
Eastman (L.)	6	2	13	0		—	—	—	—
O'Connor	15.4	8	13	3		18.3	9	34	5
Wade	4	2	10	0		—	—	—	—
H. W. Franklin	3	1	11	0		—	—	—	—
Hipkin	20	12	25	5		23	11	27	4

Umpires : Hardstaff and Phillips.

SURREY

13, 14, 15 May 1931 at The Oval

In a match that was unfortunately restricted to two days when rain prevented any play on the third day, there were many incidents to be remembered by those fortunate to be present.

On the first morning Somerset found themselves 35 for 4 as a result of some outstanding bowling by E.J. Sheffield. Young, Ingle, Jack Lee and Burrough's activities were soon over for the day. Sheffield, playing in only his second match for Surrey, succeeded in taking 4 wickets for only 4 runs from 39 balls and was later to take a further 3 wickets.

White and Case stemmed the fall of wickets, with Case playing yet another fine innings in his own peculiar style. In all he batted for 3 hours and twenty and scored 155 – his highest score for Somerset. With White he added 95 and with big-hitting Guy Earle scoring 55 out of 79 and further help from the tail, Somerset posted 338. Sheffield ended with figures of 7 for 123.

There was time for Surrey to begin their innings and Somerset must have regretted dropping Jack Hobbs when he had only scored 3. The opening pair had scored 67 by close of play. The first wicket did not fall until the Surrey score had reached 231, when Hobbs was caught at the wicket from the bowling of Wellard. Although he was dropped twice, Hobbs was still in majestic form as indeed was Sandham, who was on 131 before being caught by Young again off Wellard.

This was just the beginning of what was to become a run feast with the Surrey captain having one of his 'good' days. He went on to score 139 out of 181 in only 80 minutes after yet another dropped catch when he had scored only 10. He and the Surrey supporters enjoyed his good fortune and this was his only mistake in a glorious innings that enabled him to declare 579 for 4.

The six Somerset bowlers were given rough treatment, but sadly the rain came before Somerset were given the opportunity of batting a second time.

P.G.H. Fender batting.

Somerset v. Surrey.

PLAYED AT THE OVAL,

WEDNESDAY, THURSDAY and FRIDAY, MAY 13th, 14th and 15th, 1931.

Abandoned.

SOMERSET.

Young c Ducat b Sheffield	...	20
R. A. Ingle b Sheffield ..	...	0
Lee (J.) b Sheffield ...	...	0
H. D. Burrough b Sheffield	...	8
J. C. White c Fender b Sheffield	...	41
C. C. Case c Brooks b Gover	...	155
Wellard b Sheffield ...	...	0
G. F. Earle b Gover ...	...	55
L. Hawkins b Gover ...	...	10
Linney not out ...	...	35
Pratten c Shepherd b Sheffield	...	0
Extras	...	14
Total	...	338

SURREY.

Hobbs c. Pratten b Wellard	...	128
Sandham c Young b Wellard	...	131
Ducat c Hawkins b White	...	83
Shepherd b White ...	...	5
D. R. Jardine not out ...	...	80
P. G. H. Fender not out ...	..	139
Extras	..	13
Total (4 wkts.) *579		

* Innings declared closed.

Gregory, Peach, Brooks, Sheffield and Gover did not bat.

Bowling Analysis.

SOMERSET.			O	M	R	W
Gover	...	...	23	2	99	3
Sheffield	...	...	34.4	3	123	7
Gregory	...	...	15	5	38	0
Peach	...	...	11	4	31	0
P. G. H. Fender	...	10	0	33	0

Gover bowled 1 wide and 1 n-b.

SURREY.						
Wellard	...	...	46	7	189	2
Lee	...	...	42	6	148	0
White	...	...	44	17	110	2
Young	...	...	17	2	54	0
Hawkins	...	...	9	1	30	0
Linney	...	...	9	2	35	0

Wellard bowled 1 wide.

Umpires—Morton and Young

GLOUCESTERSHIRE
27, 28, 29 May 1931 at Bristol

Eleven years previously Gloucestershire had been dismissed for 22 by Somerset and yet somehow managed to win the match. It was now their turn to exact revenge and they proceeded to bowl out Somerset for 31. Sadly, bad weather intervened and prevented a definite result but at least there was some satisfaction for the Gloucestershire supporters.

Batting first, Gloucestershire were faced with some excellent bowling by White who took 3 of the first 4 wickets to fall and at lunch their total had lurched to 81 for 4. Things rapidly changed when Dacre came to the wicket – his 63 runs were scored in even time – and the final score of 214 would have been higher but for an unfortunate run-out. A straight drive by Dacre was deflected onto the stumps by White with Neale out of his ground, and a promising partnership was broken.

The weather then reared its ugly head and play ended for the day at 207 for 7. No play was possible on the second day and conditions were far from ideal when Gloucestershire resumed their innings on the third morning. Their 3 remaining wickets fell for the addition of only 7 runs and it was then Somerset's turn to face the music.

A disastrous start saw 3 wickets fall for only 4 runs before rain once again interrupted play. The game was obviously spoilt but Gloucestershire were keen to continue and by 4 p.m. the pitch was deemed fit for play. Somerset then suffered one of their worst batting failures and declined from 27 for 5 to 31 all out, with Parker taking 5 wickets for 11 runs and Walter Hammond, proving once again what a fine bowler he was, taking 4 for 10 off 15 overs.

The follow-on naturally took place and Ingle was soon dismissed, but Young and White steadied the ship and for an hour rebuffed all efforts from the Gloucestershire bowlers. Young was finally dismissed by Parker and immediately after this the rain came back and an incredible day's play was over.

W.R. Hammond.

Somerset v. Gloucestershire.

PLAYED AT BRISTOL,

WEDNESDAY, THURSDAY and FRIDAY, MAY 27th, 28th and 29th, 1931.

Drawn.

GLOUCESTERSHIRE.

Dipper b Lee (J.)	22
Sinfield c Earle b White	21
Hammond c & b White	11
B. H. Lyon c Wellard b White ...	1
Neale run out	14
Dacre c Marshall b White ...	64
Barnett c White b Young ...	38
Smith c Burrough b Young ...	28
Stephens c Earle b Young ...	4
Parker not out	0
Goddard c Earle b Lee	0
Extras ...	11
Total	**214**

SOMERSET.

First Innings.		Second Innings.	
Young c & b Hammond	2	l-b-w b Parker ...	19
R. A. Ingle c & b Sinfield	0	c Smith b Parker ...	2
Lee (J.) c Stephens b Parker ...	14	not out	9
L. P. Marshall b Hammond ...	0		
J. C. White c Smith b Hammond ...	1		
C. C. Case c Hammond b Parker ...	7		
G. F. Earle c Sinfield b Parker ...	3		
Wellard c Goddard b Parker ...	0		
H. G. Burrough c Smith b Parker ...	0		
Linney b Hammond	0		
Pratten not out	0		
Extras ...	4	Extras ...	6
Total	**31**	**Total (2 wkts.)**	**36**

Bowling Analysis.

GLOUCESTERSHIRE.	O	M	R	W
Wellard	17	3	36	—
Lee	30.1	16	40	2
J. C. White ...	36	9	112	4
Young	11	4	15	3

	First Innings.					Second Innings.			
SOMERSET.	O	M	R	W		O	M	R	W
Sinfield ...	3	1	6	1	...	1	—	1	—
Hammond ...	15	8	10	4	...	6	2	13	—
Parker ...	12.2	8	11	5	...	12.2	6	8	2
Goddard ...	—	—	—	—	...	6	3	6	—
Neale ...	—	—	—	—	...	1	—	2	—

Parker bowled 1 n-b.　　　　　Parker bowled 1 n-b.

Umpires—Beet and Walden.

KENT

28, 29, 30 June 1933 at Tunbridge Wells

This was a game to be remembered for the fine batting display by Jack Lee and a magnificent innings by Frank Woolley, plus extraordinarily good bowling by Freeman for Kent and Wellard for Somerset.

A first innings total of 215 by Somerset was only made possible by Jack Lee's 77. Freeman took the bowling honours with 7 wickets for 61 from 45 overs. He kept a remarkably good length and for once managed to take his wicket without the help from Les Ames behind the stumps.

Kent were soon in trouble with all their star batsmen falling to Wellard and Jack Lee. They were indeed, lucky to top the 100 as catches were dropped at vital times. With a lead of 110, Somerset set about scoring as quickly as possible and the Lee brothers saw the 100 up before they were parted. Sound batting down the order gave them the opportunity of declaring and when the score reached 277 for 8 it was duly taken.

Needing 388 for victory, Kent got off to a dreadful start losing Fairservice and Fagg with only 10 runs on the board. Enter one of the greatest batsmen of the twentieth century, Frank Woolley. Having recently recovered from a serious operation, he proceeded to play one of his greatest innings. In 270 minutes he scored 198* out of 324, playing with all of his old fluency with shots only he could play. He hit 1 six and 24 fours and with, firstly, Ames he added 101 – Ames scored 25 – and with Chapman, 91 in 55 minutes.

With Chapman still at the crease, there was every possibility of a surprise Kent victory but on his dismissal the last 4 wickets fell for only 39 runs and Somerset were worthy winners by 24 runs.

Jack Lee had a wonderful match. He scored 133 runs in the two innings and took 6 for 134 with his slow bowling, but the honours really went to Woolley for his 198* – he did not deserve to be on the losing side.

Jack Lee.

Arthur Fagg (left) and Frank Woolley.

Somerset *v.* Kent.

PLAYED AT TUNBRIDGE WELLS,

Wednesday, Thursday and Friday, June 28th, 29th and 30th, 1933.

Somerset won by 24 runs.

SOMERSET.

First Innings.			Second Innings.		
Lee (J. W.) c Chapman b Freeman ...		77	c & b Hardinge	...	56
Lee (F. S.) l-b-w b Valentine	...	3	b Hardinge	...	44
C. C. Case run out ...	....	1	b Todd ...	...	20
J. W. Seamer b Freeman ...	...	14	b Watt ...	...	8
Young b Freeman ...	...	0	c Watt b Freeman	...	48
R. A. Ingle l-b-w b Freeman	...	45	b Watt ...	...	27
H. D. Burrough l-b-w b Freeman	...	10	c & b Valentine	...	8
Wellard c Valentine b Freeman	...	0	not out ...	...	30
G. M. Bennett hit wkt b Freeman	...	29	run out ..	...	2
Luckes not out	...	12	not out ...	...	7
Hazell c Watt b Hardinge	...	8			
Extras ...		16	Extras ...		27
Total		215	Total (8 wkts.)		*277

*Innings declared closed.

KENT.

First Innings.			Second Innings.		
Fairservice b Wellard	...	4	c Luckes b Wellard		1
Fagg b Wellard	...	4.	b Wellard ...	...	0
Woolley b Wellard	...	4	b Lee (J. W.)	...	198
Ames b Lee (J. W.)	..	10	c Luckes b Young	...	25
Todd b Lee (J. W.)	...	10	c & b Hazell	...	17
B. H. Valentine c Young b Wellard ...		0	b Young ..	...	10
Hardinge c Seamer b Lee (J. W.)	...	36	c Lee (F. S. b Wellard		22
A. P. F. Chapman c Luckes b Wellard		18	c Young b Lee (J. W.)		53
Watt c Lee (F. S.) b Wellard	...	0	c Young b Lee (J. W.)		0
Freeman not out	..	13	not out ...	..	12
Wright c Hazell b Wellard	...	0	run out ...	...	10
Extras ...		6	Extras ...		15
Total		105	Total		363

Bowling Analysis.

SOMERSET.		First Innings.					Second Innings.			
		O	M	R	W		O	M	R	W
Watt	...	26	10	52	—	...	27	6	79	2
B. H. Valentine	...	7	3	6	1	...	11	2	44	1
Freeman	...	45	24	61	7	...	25	11	61	1
Wright	...	15	3	37	—	...	8	1	19	—
Hardinge	...	24.3	11	43	1	...	12	4	24	2
Todd	...	—	—	—	—	...	4	1	19	1
Fairservice	...	—	—	—	—	...	1	—	4	—

Watt bowled 2 n-b. Watt 1 n-b. Valentine 2 wds. Wright 1 wide.

KENT.										
Wellard	...	21.4	3	59	7	...	22.4	4	141	3
Lee (J. W.)	...	21	7	40	3	...	34	9	94	3
Young	...	—	—	—	—	...	29	5	68	2
Hazell	...	—	—	—	—	...	15	3	45	1

Wellard and Lee (J. W.) 1 wide each. Wellard 2 n-b. Lee (J. W.) 1 n-b.

Umpires—Chester and Hardstaff.

GLOUCESTERSHIRE

26, 28, 29 May 1934 at Bristol

This local 'derby' was one of the best for many years with each side appearing to have the upper hand during three days of exciting cricket. The extremely dry weather in April and May had made it difficult for the groundsmen to produce good wickets and this one was far from perfect when Somerset found themselves batting on the opening day.

Excluding Jack Lee, who was caught behind the wicket off Barnett, the next seven batsman all got a start but it was stubborn batting by Frank Lee, with 46, and Arthur Wellard's 47 that ensured Somerset reached at least 200. That wily off-spinner Tom Goddard took 4 wickets and Gloucestershire were the happier of the two teams.

Without Hammond, Gloucestershire were hoping that Barnett and Sinfield would see off the opening bowling of Wellard and Buse but the introduction of White into the attack changed the picture dramatically – he dismissed them both and was extremely accurate which made scoring very difficult. Jack Lee was a good foil and had it not been for a most impressive innings by D.A.C. Page, the hosts would have fallen far short of Somerset's total. His 83 contained 14 boundaries and with Neale he appeared to have turned the game in Gloucestershire's favour.

On batting a second time Somerset came up against Goddard at his best. His final figures of 7 for 71 from 30 overs would have been even better had two catches not been dropped, but 'Box' Case came to the rescue. Whilst his style left a lot to be desired, he went on to make 106* in a total of only 192 and with G.M. Bennett turned the game in Somerset's favour – they had been 37 for 7.

As Gloucestershire needed 153 to win, they were in difficulties from the start. Wickets fell to Jack Lee and Jack White and they were soon 30 for 5. A late effort by Neale, with support from Cranfield, failed to meet the challenge and Somerset were worthy winners by 37 runs.

Jack Lee had match figures of 9 for 163 and Jack White 11 for 136, and they thoroughly deserved to be on the winning side.

C.C.C. Case.

Somerset *v.* Gloucestershire.

PLAYED AT BRISTOL,

SATURDAY, MONDAY and TUESDAY, MAY 26th, 28th and 29th, 1934.

Somerset won by 39 runs.

SOMERSET.

First Innings.		Second Innings.	
Lee (J. W.) c Hopkins b Barnett ...	0	c Dacre b Goddard ...	14
Lee (F. S.) c Hopkins b Goddard ...	46	b Goddard ...	3
R. A. Ingle l-b-w b Sinfield ...	18	st Hopkins b Parker ...	0
E. F. Longrigg c Goddard b Cranfield	32	c Cranfield b Goddard	1
C. C. Case b Goddard	21	not out	106
L. Hawkins c Goddard b Cranfield ...	23	b Goddard ...	0
Wellard c Barnett b Sinfield ...	47	c Lyon b Parker ..	0
J. C. White c Dacre b Goddard ..	21	c Goddard b Parker ...	6
G. M. Bennett b Goddard ...	4	c Cranfield b Goddard	54
Luckes c Neale b Lyon ...	5	b Goddard ...	1
Buse not out	3	c Allen b Goddard ...	0
Extras ...	5	Extras ...	7
Total	225	Total	192

GLOUCESTERSHIRE.

First Innings.		Second Innings.	
Barnett c Wellard b White ...	22	c Hawkins b Lee (J. W.)	13
Sinfield c Hawkins b White ...	33	b Lee (J. W.) ...	10
B. H. Lyon b Lee (J. W.) ...	19	c Buse b Lee (J. W.) ...	7
B. O. Allen c Buse b White ...	11	c & b White ...	0
Dacre c Ingle b Lee (J. W.) ...	9	b Lee (J. W.) ...	0
D. A. C. Page l-b-w b White ...	83	c & b White ...	11
Neale st Luckes b Lee (J. W.) ...	49	c Lee (J. W.) b White...	39
Hopkins c Wellard b White ...	8	b Lee (J. W.) ...	0
Parker c Bennett b White ...	20	l-b-w b White ...	2
Cranfield st Luckes b Lee (J. W.) ..	5	not out	16
Goddard not out	6	c Lee (F. S.) b White ...	4
Extras ...	10	Extras ...	1
Total	275	Total	103

Bowling Analysis.

SOMERSET.		First Innings.					Second Innings.			
		O	M	R	W		O	M	R	W
Barnett	...	12	3	21	1	...	—	—	—	—
Sinfield	...	23	6	48	2	...	6	·	22	—
Parker	...	8	2	19	—	...	25	5	82	3
Goddard	...	26.4	10	54	4	...	30	6	71	7
Cranfield	...	16	1	74	2	...	3	1	10	—
B. H. Lyon	—	2	—	4	1	...	—	—	—	—

Parker bowled 1 n-b.

GLOUCESTERSHIRE.										
Wellard	...	9	1	42	—	...	—	—	—	—
Buse	...	8	1	26	—	...	—	—	—	—
J. C. White	...	46	15	96	6	...	26.1	10	40	5
Lee (J. W.)	...	37	10	101	4	...	27	10	62	5

Wellard bowled 4 n-b.

Umpires—Baldwin and Stone.

Essex

18, 20, 21 May 1935 at Frome

This was a game that aroused more interest and was more widely reported than any other County game in the 1930s. A young Somerset all-rounder, originally rejected by his County, found himself the centre of attraction. A last-minute choice largely because there was no one else available was to become a celebrity overnight. He even had to 'hitch' a lift to the match and he was fortunate that Somerset had won the toss and had elected to bat.

Finding himself number eight in the batting order came as no surprise, but he did not have too long to wait before he had to make his way to the middle. Somerset were in a precarious position having lost 6 wickets in scoring only 107 when he set off from the pavilion with a borrowed bat to face the strong Essex attack. He treated all the bowlers, including Nicholls, who was a current Test player, with scant respect and scored his first 50 in just 28 minutes.

His stroke play was audacious, with shots all around the wicket, driving, pulling, hooking, even late cutting and it was hard to believe that he was not a seasoned professional in extravagant mood! Whilst it was a small ground, nothing could be taken away from his 3 sixes and 17 fours. He went on to score 123 before being caught and bowled by Eastman. His runs were scored out of 175 in only 80 minutes with his century coming after 63 minutes which was to be the fastest century of the season making him the winner of the Lawrence trophy.

Help from Bill Andrews, who scored 71, saw Somerset total 337 after Gimblett's heroics came to an end at 282. Andrews hit 3 sixes and 7 fours which kept the large crowd happy and the scorers busy. Nicholls took 6 wickets, but his performance was completely overshadowed by the debutant's batting.

Play was impossible on the second day owing to rain and a Somerset victory was in doubt, even though they had secured 5 Essex wickets for 87 in the time available on the first day.

Jack Lee and Arthur Wellard soon disposed of the last 5 wickets when play began again, though a stubborn innings by O'Connor delayed them and saw Essex reach 141. The follow-on was enforced and once again Jack Lee's slow bowling helped his side to victory by 49 runs. In all he took 9 wickets – 4 for 26 and 5 for 67 – but the match will always be remembered as Gimblett's debut.

Harold Gimblett.

Harold Gimblett's Hundred

by John Arlott

Bicknoller was his village, Harold Gimblett was his name
Farming was his working day, but cricket was his game.
When he was but twenty, and first played for Somerset
He played the mighty innings that we remember yet.

CHORUS:
>   *Oh, he struck them with skill and he struck them with power,*
>   *Times out of number*
>   *He gave them Stogumber*
>   *And knocked up a hundred in just on the hour.*

Stogumber is the village where Jack White used to live;
But for cricketers in Somerset, that's the name they give
To the fierce cross-batted stroke they will use for ever more,
Swinging it right off the stumps and past long leg for four.

Young Gimblett went to Taunton to have a county trial.
John Daniel broke the news to him, they did not like his style.
Then a man cried off, and he was called back to the room
'You'll play for tomorrow, against Essex down at Frome.'

On May the eighteenth, 'thirty-five, at six he left the farm
On the way to catch the bus, cricket bag under his arm.
Soon to drink pavilion tea, though he felt a little grim,
With cricketers who up till then had been but names to him.

Somerset had Ingle, the two Lees, Frank and Jack,
The famous Farmer White and Arthur Wellard in attack.
For Essex, Pearce, O'Connor, the Smiths, Peter and Ray,
Eastman, Wade and Cutmore, they all were there that day.

There was Nichols of England too, the mighty 'Maurice Nick',
His arms were long, his shoulders wide, his pace was mighty quick.
When Somerset went in to bat, his slips held all the snicks.
The score when Gimblett's turn came round was One-O-Seven for Six.

The crowd had never heard of him, they did not know his name,
But since he was for Somerset they clapped him just the same;
They saw him miss the spin of Smith but very quickly then
For a single pushed off Nicholls they clapped him again.

In Arthur Wellard, biggest hitter of them all,
Young Gimblett soon outscored him – he was middling the ball.
When Smith tossed up his googly – that ball of mystery –
He landed it Stogumber on top of the old marquee.

Wellard went and Luckes came. Gimblett reached his fifty.
Luckes went, Bill Andrews then played it cool and thrifty.
Nichols took the bright new ball and Gimblett drove him straight,
When he dropped it short he hooked him, and cut him neat and late.

The chilly crowd had watched him while he had changed the game,
And now they felt they knew him and they shouted out his name.
For one fine savage over, Nichols checked his score,
But then the young man cracked him through the old pavilion door.

A difficult situation fell on the Frome ground then,
Because the tins there only marked the score up ten by ten.
Of tension in the dressing room, the team could give no sign,
There was no way of telling him his score was ninety-nine.

But Nichols bowled and Gimblett then drove him clean for four
He'd done it – scored a century – the crowd let out a roar,
And to this day you may read it, it's in the record book,
An hour and just three minutes was all the time he took.

That night, all through Somerset, from Minehead 'cross to Street,
Bristol down to Wellington, they talked of this great feat;
And thousands ever since have claimed that they were there to see
Harold Gimblett, from Bicknoller, make cricket history.

Frome cricket ground.

Somerset *v.* Essex.

PLAYED AT FROME,

SATURDAY, MONDAY and TUESDAY, MAY 18th, 20th and 21st, 1935.

Somerset won by an Innings and 49 runs.

SOMERSET.

Lee (J. W.) c Eastman b Nichols	...	3
Lee (F. S.) lbw b Nichols	...	41
R. A. Ingle c Eastman b Nichols	...	12
J. C. White c Eastman b Nichols	...	4
C. C. Case b Smith (P.) ...	...	35
H. D. Burrough b Nichols	...	2
Wellard st Wade b Evans	...	21
Gimblett c & b Eastman	...	123
Luckes b Nichols ..	...	7
Andrews c O'Conner b Evans	...	71
Hazell not out ...	...	7
Extras ...		11
Total		**337**

ESSEX.

First Innings.			Second Innings.	
Cutmore lbw b Wellard ...	...	24	b Lee (J. W.) ...	26
Rist c Lee (J. W.) b Wellard	...	41	c Wellard b Hazell ...	21
T. N. Pearce b Wellard ...	...	1	st Luckes b Hazell ...	0
O'Conner not out ...	...	30	c Burrough b Wellard...	25
Nichols c Lee (J. W.) b Wellard	...	0	st Luckes b White ...	31
T. P. Lawrence b Wellard	...	4	b Lee (J. W.) ...	6
Eastman b Lee (J. W.) ...	...	35	lbw b White ..	1
Smith (P.) b Lee (J. W.) ...	...	0	c Ingle b Lee (J. W.) ...	22
Wade c Wellard b Hazell ...	...	1	lbw b Lee (J. W.) ...	9
Evans c Wellard b Lee (J. W.	...	2	st Luckes b Lee (J. W.)	1
Smith (R.) lbw (N) b Lee (J. W.)	...	0	not out	0
Extras ...		3	Extras	5
Total		**141**	**Total**	**147**

Bowling Analysis.

SOMERSET.		O	M	R	W
Nichols ...	...	23	3	87	6
Smith (R.)...	...	13	2	43	—
Eastman ...	..	13	4	38	1
Evans ...	...	14.5	1	69	2
Smith (P.) ...	...	13	1	89	1

Nichols 1 wd.

ESSEX.		First Innings.					Second Innings.			
		O	M	R	W		O	M	R	W
Wellard	...	23	6	66	5	...	9	2	18	1
Andrews	...	7	1	20	—	...	1	—	5	—
J. C. White	...	16	8	16	—	...	15	4	31	2
Lee (J. W.)	...	10	1	26	4	...	21.5	5	67	5
Hazell	...	11	8	10	1	...	10	4	21	2

Wellard 1 n-b.

Umpires—Chester and Dipper

SURREY

9, 10, 11 June 1937 at The Oval

This was a game that produced outstanding bowling figures for Bill Andrews, although Somerset still managed to lose it. A June storm changed the pattern of the game and a previously normal Oval wicket was to become a minefield with the ball darting around at varying heights after two days of predictable flatness.

Surrey established a first-innings lead of 140 with centuries by Gregory and Squires in a total of 406. By the end of the second day Somerset had lost 7 wickets and after the overnight rain and early morning sunshine they quickly lost the remaining three.

When it was Surrey's turn to bat, the wicket was at its worst and within an hour they were dismissed for 35 with Bill Andrews taking 8 wickets including a hat-trick – Fishlock, Parker and Brookes – as well as being hit for 6 by Barling.

It was Surrey's lowest score since 1893 and Andrews had achieved his remarkable figures in just 40 balls; some forty years later he was still moaning about a dropped catch on the boundary that enabled Barling to record his 6. Could his final analysis have been 9 for 6 rather than 8 for 12?

With plenty of time left Somerset required 178 runs to win, but once again a weak batting display followed and they failed to meet the challenge. With 15 minutes' batting time remaining before lunch they lost the all-important wicket of Frank Lee and whilst the wicket was by now much easier, they had no answer to the fast bowling of Alf Gover. Seven wickets fell for only 43 runs and all the established batsmen were back in the pavilion.

Denied bowling success, Arthur Wellard was to prove his worth as a batsman and though dropped twice he hit 2 towering sixes off Freddie Brown and, with help from Luckes and Hazell, a Somerset victory became a possibility. Hazell finally succumbed to Gover but not before the 9th wicket had added 67 and by now only 29 runs were required. The last man, an amateur, P.S.M. Molyneux, did his best and defended stoutly, giving the strike to Wellard whenever possible, but for reasons unknown Wellard went into his shell and runs were reduced to a trickle.

The partnership got to within 11 runs of victory when Wellard decided that Molyneux could not be expected to survive a further over from Gover; after a mid-wicket conference it was decided that come what may a run would be attempted from the last ball of the over bowled by Watts. Disaster struck when an almost wide ball eluded Wellard, but wicketkeeper Brookes had an easy task in defeating Molyneux's vain effort to reach safety. It was all over with Wellard ending up the villain rather than the hero.

Far left: A.W. Wellard. Left: W.H.R. Andrews.

Somerset *v.* Surrey.

PLAYED AT THE OVAL,

WEDNESDAY, THURSDAY and FRIDAY, JUNE 9th, 10th and 11th, 1937

Somerset lost by 11 runs.

SURREY.

First Innings.		Second Innings.	
D. J. Knight c Luckes b Andrews ...	3	c & b Andrews ...	2
Sandham b Kinnersley	56	c Ingle b Andrews ...	1
Gregory c & b Kinnersley	102	hit wicket b Wellard ...	0
Squires c Luckes b Wellard ...	116	c Lee b Andrews ...	2
Barling c Hazell b Kinnersley ...	53	c Hazell b Wellard ...	6
Fishlock b Wellard	11	c Lee b Wellard ...	9
F. R. Brown c Hazell b Wellard ...	17	c Burrough b Andrews ...	0
Parker not out	18	c Hazell b Andrews ...	6
Watts c Hazell b Andrews... ...	1	c & b Andrews ...	9
Brooks b Wellard	16	c Hazell b Andrews ...	0
Gover b Andrews	2	not out	0
Extras ...	11	Extras ...	0
Total	**406**	**Total**	**35**

SOMERSET.

Lee (F. S.) c Knight b Brown ...	130	c Brown b Watts ...	2
L. Hawkins c Brooks b Brown ...	12	c Brooks b Watts ...	4
H. D. Burrough c Brooks b Gover ...	27	c & b Gover ...	10
K. C. Kinnersley b Squires ...	9	lbw b Gover ...	2
Andrews b Gover	28	b Watts	16
C. J. P. Barnwell b Brown... ...	5	b Gover	1
R. A. Ingle c & b Gover	21	c Squires b Gover ...	7
Wellard lbw b Brown	9	not out	91
Luckes not out	9	lbw b Squires ...	18
P. S. M. Molyneux b Brown ...	0	run out	3
Hazell c Knight b Brown	5	b Gover	6
Extras ...	9	Extras ...	6
Total	**264**	**Total**	**166**

Bowling Analysis

		First Innings.				Second Innings.		
SURREY.		O	M	R	W	O	M	R	W
Wellard	...	39	4	128	4	...	7	1	23	2
Andrews	...	35.1	4	118	3	...	6.4	2	12	8
Hazell	...	15	—	62	—	...	—	—	—	—
K. C. Kinnersley	...	23	6	61	3	...	—	—	—	—
L. Hawkins	...	5	—	26	—	...	1	—	1	—

Andrews 1 wide.

SOMERSET.		O	M	R	W	O	M	R	W
Gover	...	32	3	93	3	...	20	7	48	5
Watts	...	20	6	38	—	...	18	2	73	3
Parker	...	13	3	31	—	...	—	—	—	—
F. R. Brown	...	26	3	77	6	...	5	1	36	—
Squires	...	12	6	16	1	...	3	1	3	1

Gover 1 n-b.
Gover 1 wide and 2 n-b.
Umpires—Smith and Smart

GLOUCESTERSHIRE
4, 6, 7 June 1938 at Taunton

Another thriller that had spectators on the edge of their seats with one of the most exciting finishes seen at Taunton for many years. The final result, a victory for Somerset by 1 wicket, had been far from certain, but once again Wellard turned the tables with an innings of 68.

Gloucestershire batted first and had struggled to 221 with the new England captain, Walter Hammond, scoring only 6, but wicketkeeper Andy Wilson helped them to reach 200. Hazell was the pick of the Somerset bowlers, taking 4 for 42.

Somerset got off to a good start, with openers Gimblett and Frank Lee each scoring a half-century and 'Dar' Lyon was only two short of following suit when he was dismissed. Scott, a new fast bowler, took 4 wickets and one could see why he was being regarded as a possible England bowler of the future. He helped restrain Somerset's total to 276 – a lead of 55.

Barnett and Emmett were soon out, both to Wellard, but it was not often that Hammond failed twice in the same match and this was no exception. He treated a good crowd to one of his finest displays, batting 270 minutes for an amazing 140*. Gloucestershire's Lyon helped him in an 8th-wicket stand of 161 and the declaration came with the score on 338 for 7, a lead of 283.

The challenge started badly with Gimblett out for only 7, and wickets continued to tumble. Bertie Buse was the exception playing one of his best innings in scoring 79, but the 7th wicket fell with only 161 on the board – a further 112 was required for victory. Enter Arthur Wellard, who once again came to the rescue with an audacious innings of 68, which included 6 sixes and

5 fours scored in 40 minutes and the pendulum had swung in Somerset's favour.

However, in spite of Wellard's onslaught, time now entered the equation, and it was thanks to Wally Luckes that a Somerset victory was finally achieved. When the last over of the day began, all results were possible but Luckes made sure by hitting 2 fours off Sinsfield, the second from the 4th ball of the over.

Gloucestershire had tried 7 bowlers, but without the services of Goddard, who was injured, they were always struggling to prevent Somerset from winning this thrilling match.

Arthur Wellard.

Somerset *v.* Gloucestershire.

PLAYED AT TAUNTON,

SATURDAY, MONDAY and TUESDAY, JUNE 4th, 6th and 7th, 1938.

Somerset won by 1 wicket.

GLOUCESTERSHIRE.

First Innings			Second Innings		
B. O. Allen c Lyon b Hazell	...	52	run out		28
Barnett l-b-w b Wellard ...	...	41	c & b Wellard ...		0
Emmett b Wellard ..	...	18	l-b-w b Wellard ..		6
W. R. Hammond c Luckes b Hazell ...		6	not out		140
Crapp b Buse ...	...	33	b Wellard ...		29
Neale c Luckes b Hazell ...	..	13	c Luckes b Wellard ...		6
B. H. Lyon c Gimblett b Hazell ...		0	c Longrigg b Hazell ...		88
Sinfield b Wellard ...	...	0	not out		0
Wilson b Andrews ...	...	38	c Andrews b Kinnersley		32
Scott l-b-w b Andrews ...	...	9			
Cranfield not out ...	...	5			
Extras ...		6	Extras ...		9
Total 221			* Total (7 wkts.) 338		

* Innings declared closed.

SOMERSET.

First Innings			Second Innings		
Lee (F.) l-b-w b Sinfield ...	...	56	c Allen b Barnett ...		18
Gimblett c Wilson b Emmett ...		67	c Allen b Sinfield ...		7
M. D. Lyon b Hammond ...	...	48	l-b-w b Barnett ...		19
Buse c Wilson b Scott ...	...	27	c Emmett b Hammond		79
E. F. Longrigg c Hammond b Sinfield		7	b Sinfield		24
J. W. Seamer c Allen b Scott ...		23	run out		34
Andrews c Wilson b Barnett ...		6	c Barnett b Emmett ...		2
K. C. Kinnersley c Allen b Scott ...		12	c & b Emmett ...		7
Wellard b Hammond ...	...	21	c Barnett b Scott ...		68
Luckes l-b-w b Scott ..	..	2	not out		18
Hazell not out ...	...	0	not out		0
Extras ...		7	Extras ...		8
Total 276			Total (for 9 wkts.) 284		

Bowling Analysis.

GLOUCESTERSHIRE.	First Innings.					Second Innings.			
	O	M	R	W		O	M	R	W
Wellard ..	30	6	77	3	..	32	7	85	4
Andrews ..	15.1	—	48	2	..	16	1	76	—
Buse ...	17	4	48	1	...	27	6	86	—
Hazell ...	16	2	42	4	...	27	6	72	1
Kinnersley ..	—	—	—	—	..	5	2	10	1

Hazell 1 wide. Buse 1 n-b- Wellard 2 n-b.

SOMERSET.									
W. R. Hammond ...	33.2	8	64	2	...	17	3	57	1
Scott ..	19	2	42	4	..	15	3	51	1
Sinfield ...	39	20	57	2	...	29.4	10	68	2
Barnett ...	10	1	21	1	...	17	5	50	2
Cranfield ...	6	—	33	—	...	2	—	5	—
Emmett ...	9	1	52	1	...	6	..	36	2
Neale ...	—	—	—	—	...	2	—	9	—

Cranfield 1 wide. Hammond 1 n-b. Umpires— Dolphin and Robinson.

WORCESTERSHIRE

17, 18, 19 August 1938 at Worcester

Yet another match against Worcestershire provided interest of a different kind. Frank Lee completed a not-out century in Somerset's first innings and was not out in the second innings when the 9th wicket fell. Would he be able to equal a long-standing record held by C.J.B. Wood, who scored two not-out centuries when opening the innings against Yorkshire in 1911?

The first Worcestershire innings gave the impression that it would be a low-scoring match when Arthur Wellard took the first 6 wickets to fall at a modest cost. Worcestershire never really recovered, although Martin stayed long enough to help the score along to 146. Wellard finished with very good figures, 7 for 59, a just reward for some splendid bowling.

Runs were still hard to get when Somerset batted but Frank Lee and Bill Andrews, in his elevated batting position at number three, kept the scoreboard ticking over and Andrews had scored 49 before he was run out chasing his 50. The slump then began with only Barnwell managing double figures after being dropped twice in getting 18. Thanks to Lee carrying his bat for a gallant 109, Somerset obtained a lead of 50 runs.

A much better batting performance was to follow, Hon. C.J. Lyttleton with 75 (including 2 sixes and 13 fours) in 50 minutes, Gibbons 69 and Howorth 52 ensured that Somerset would have to bat well to score 251 to win.

Victory always appeared to be beyond them, particularly after Gimblett was out for 20 and the next 6 wickets fell quickly, but the interest was maintained by Frank Lee's presence at the crease. Tension grew as Wellard fell to a catch off Howorth and A.A. Pearse was dismissed without scoring. Lee reached his century and with the reliable number eleven, Hazell, defending stoutly, it was strange that Somerset supporters were in fact hoping that Hazell would soon succumb to the Worcestershire bowlers. It was not to be. Tragedy struck and Lee was caught Singleton bowled Martin for 107. He had been on the pitch for the whole game but sadly failed in his attempt to equal Wood's record which was to remain intact until 1991, when Jimmy Cook scored his 2 not-out centuries against Nottinghamshire at Trent Bridge.

Frank Lee.

R. Howorth.

Somerset *v.* Worcestershire.

PLAYED AT WORCESTER,
WEDNESDAY, THURSDAY and FRIDAY, AUGUST 17th, 18th and 19th, 1938.

Somerset lost by 45 runs.

WORCESTERSHIRE.

First Innings.		Second Innings.	
Hon. C. J. Lyttelton b Wellard ...	18	c Hazell b Andrews ...	75
Howorth l-b-w b Wellard	20	c Gimblett b Wellard...	52
Cooper b Wellard	2	b Hazell ...	16
Nawab of Pataudi b Wellard ...	0	c Wellard b Andrews...	14
Gibbons c Gimblett b Wellard ...	21	c Gimblett b Wellard ...	69
Martin c Luckes b Andrews · :..	32	c Gimblett b Wellard ...	22
C. D. A. Pullan b Wellard ...	16	b Hazell	11
A. P. Singleton c Wellard b Buse ...	11	not out	24
Buller b Wellard	19	c Lyon b Hazell ...	1
Jenkins b Andrews	4	b Hazell	0
Perks not out	1	b Hazell -... ...	3
Extras ...	2	Extras ...	13
Total	**146**	**Total**	**300**

SOMERSET.

First Innings.		Second Innings.	
Lee (F.) not out	109	c Singleton b Martin ...	107
Gimblett c Buller b Perks	0	c Gibbons b Howorth...	20
Andrews run out	49	c Buller b Howorth ...	12
Buse b Jenkins	1	c Pataudi b Howorth ..	3
A. T. M. Jones l-b-w b Martin ...	0	c & b Jenkins ...	0
M. D. Lyon c Perks b Jenkins ...	9	c & b Howorth ...	3
C. J. P. Barnwell c Cooper b Perks ...	18	c Perks b Howorth ...	0
Luckes b Perks	6	b Martin ...	15
Wellard c Pullan b Martin... ...	0	c Pataudi b Howorth ...	27
A. A. Pearse b Martin	0	c Singleton b Martin ...	0
Hazell b Martin	2	not out	5
Extras ...	2	Extras ...	13
Total	**196**	**Total**	**205**

Bowling Analysis

WORCESTER.	First Innings.					Second Innings.			
	O	M	R	W		O	M	R	W
Wellard ...	18.2	4	59	7	...	27	4	106	3
Andrews ...	10	2	35	2	...	26	4	81	·2
Buse ...	8	2	25	1	...	8 ·	2	29	—
Hazell ...	6	—	17	—	...	16. 2	2	50	5
M. D. Lyon ...	2	—	8	—	...	1	—	5	—
Gimblett ...	—	—	—	—	...	3	1	8	—
A. T. M. Jones ...	—	—	—	—		1	—	8	—

Wellard 1 wide & 4 n-b. Gimblett 1 wide.

SOMERSET.	O	M	R	W		O	M	R	W
Perks ...	24	3	83	3	...	16·	7	35	—
Martin ...	24.4	3	49	4 ·	...	15.4	4	48	3
Howorth ...	7	2	13	—	...	25	6	51	6
A. P. Singleton ..	10	2	33	—	..	7	2	16	—
Jenkins ·...	11	3	16	2	...	11	—	42	1

Howorth 1 wide. Perks 1 n-b.

Umpires—Dolphin and Robinson.

KENT

24, 25 August 1938 at Wells

This was a match remembered for the all-round performance of Arthur Wellard. He was born in Kent but was rejected by the County for apparently not being good enough to be a County professional cricketer. He certainly made them regret their decision over two August days in 1938 by taking 13 wickets in the match and pulverising the bowling of Frank Woolley, scoring 31 off 1 over from his bowling and being largely instrumental in Somerset's victory by 27 runs on the second day of the match.

Somerset elected to bat and produced a strange batting order with Bill Andrews at number three. The ploy worked on this small ground and Bill enjoyed himself, striking the ball to the boundary whenever possible. The real excitement came later when 'Dar' Lyon, an attacking batsman, found himself completely upstaged when at the fall of the 7th wicket Wellard strode from the small pavilion and in 37 minutes scored 57. He struck Woolley for 31 in a single over consisting of 5 sixes and a single – the latter, resulting from a dropped catch! (Wellard had previously taken 30 from an over bowled by Armstrong of Derbyshire on the same ground in 1936). The innings closed at 225.

Kent could hardly have started their innings in a more depressing way. Three wickets fell, including that of Frank Woolley, before a run had been scored, with Wellard taking two of the three. A fourth wicket was soon to follow, but when C.H. Knott joined Valentine the large crowd saw batting of the highest quality. Valentine was in superb form and the pair added 180 in well under 2 hours to give Kent some hope. Valentine hit 4 sixes and 14 fours before being stumped off the bowling of Hazell in an innings that was talked about for a long time.

Enter once again that man Wellard. He took 3 further wickets at a cost of only one run ending with 7 for 65 with Kent finding themselves 10 runs in arrears when the last wicket fell.

The small ground seemed to affect all the batsmen and more big hitting was to follow in the second innings, but wickets fell with monotonous regularity and once again it was left to Wellard to ensure that Kent were set a reasonable target. Bill Andrews top scored with

a boisterous 54 but Wellard's 37 saved the day for Somerset.

Kent were left 187 runs to get for victory, but after only 4 overs from Andrews, Wellard and Hazell set about the task of dismissing the visitors as quickly as possible. Woolley looked dangerous but fell lbw to Wellard for 34, and when Valentine was stumped for the second time in the match off Hazell, the pendulum swung in Somerset's favour. The intriguing struggle continued but with 27 runs still needed for victory the last Kent wicket fell. Wellard with 6 wickets and Hazell with 4 proved too much for the visitors.

Wellard's match figures of 13 for 115 resulted from fine bowling and together with his contribution from the bat it has been recognised in cricket history as Wellard's match.

Claude Lewis.

Arthur Wellard.

B.H. Valentine.

Somerset v. Kent.

PLAYED AT WELLS,

WEDNESDAY, THURSDAY and FRIDAY, AUGUST 24th, 25th and 26th, 1938.

Somerset won by 27 runs.

SOMERSET.

First Innings.		Second Innings.	
Lee (F.) l-b-w b Lewis	35	c Levett b Todd ...	3
Gimblett c Chalk b Todd	14	c Woolley b Harding ...	5
Andrews b Watt	30	l-b-w b Lewis ...	54
Buse c Levett b Lewis	11	b Harding ...	25
E. F. Longrigg c Levett b Lewis ...	6	b Lewis	18
M. D. Lyon not out	50	st. Levett b Woolley ...	8
G. M. Bennett b Harding	1	b Harding ...	9
Luckes c Spencer b Lewis ...	2	l-b-w b Lewis ...	4
Wellard c Harding b Todd ...	57	b Harding ...	37
A. T. M. Jones c Spencer b Lewis ...	1	c Levett b Harding ...	2
Hazell c Watt b Lewis	2	not out	0
Extras ...	16	Extras ...	12
Total	225	Total	177

KENT.

First Innings		Second Innings	
Woolley l-b-w b Wellard	0	l-b-w b Wellard ...	34
F. G. H. Chalk b Andrews ...	0	c Andrews b Hazell ...	33
Todd l-b-w b Wellard	0	c Jones b Wellard ...	13
B. H. Valentine st. Luckes b Hazell ...	114	st. Luckes b Hazell ...	13
Sunnocks c Luckes b Wellard ...	8	b Wellard ...	0
C. H. Knott c Lyon b Wellard ...	65	b Wellard ...	19
Spencer c Luckes b Wellard ...	14	st. Luckes b Wellard ...	12
W. H. V. Levett b Wellard ...	0	not out	12
Harding not out	9	c Jones b Wellard ...	6
Watt b Andrews	0	c Wellard b Hazell ...	8
Lewis b Wellard	1	b Hazell	1
Extras	4	Extras	9
Total	215	Total	160

Bowling Analysis.

		First Innings.					Second Innings.			
SOMERSET.		O	M	R	W		O	M	R	W
Todd	...	15	4	46	2	...	11	5	11	1
Harding	...	12	4	25	1	...	15.3	3	51	5
Watt	...	16	6	22	1	...	12	2	40	—
Lewis	...	25.3	4	76	6	...	21	6	57	3
Woolley	...	2	—	40	—	...	5	1	6	1

Harding 1 wide and 3 n-b.

		O	M	R	W		O	M	R	W
KENT.										
Wellard	...	25.3	8	65	7	...	27	7	50	6
Andrews	...	14	1	49	2	...	4	—	35	—
Hazell	...	17	3	67	1	...	22.2	2	60	4
Buse	...	6	1	30	—	...	1	—	6	—

Umpires—Skelding and Baldwin.

KENT

21, 22, 23 June 1939 at Bath

Kent again provided an exciting finish on their visit to the West Country. This was a low scoring game that provided entertainment and interest to a good crowd throughout the three days.

Somerset started with Frank Lee and Harold Gimblett both batting well on an easy paced wicket, and the score had reached 61 before the first wicket fell. It was the introduction of England's leg spinner, Doug Wright, that changed the game completely. In 11 overs, he took 8 for 35 on a day when he could do little wrong and when Watt bowled Wellard for 6, the innings was over with just 145 runs scored. After Gimblett's 52 it was left to Dickie Burrough with a patient 25 to help the score along, but it was a poor total on a good wicket.

Kent, with a very long tail, were hoping that their five major batsmen would see them to a large first-innings lead but Somerset had other ideas. Bill Andrews took the leading role and bowling beautifully was soon amongst the wickets. Fagg and Chalk gave Kent a reasonable start but with Foster and Valentine both falling to Andrews, the tail was soon exposed though they still managed a first-innings lead of 31.

It was much as before when Somerset batted again – Watt and Todd took the important opening wickets. These were followed by another major collapse at the hand of Doug Wright. The next seven batsmen failed to reach double figures, two failing to score at all, and the game would have been over if an easy catch given by Wellard had been held – he was actually dropped 4 times off 5 balls from Wright, but proceeded to score 48 vital runs to give Somerset a chance of victory.

Once again a third factor entered into the match – rain. On the third day, play was impossible after 4 p.m., which left Kent 75 minutes in which to score 99 runs. A much changed batting order was not successful. Fagg and Valentine, the two danger men, both failed.

P.G. Foster failed to raise the scoring rate with a rather dour 29 and Kent only managed to score 72 of the 99 required for victory, losing 7 wickets in the process.

Only 16 overs were bowled, 8 each by Wellard and Andrews, before stumps were drawn and so ended an exciting match, although the ending was perhaps a disappointing one for both sides.

Doug Wright had match figures of 16 for 80, which shows why he was feared by all County batsmen.

Doug Wright.

SOMERSET v. KENT.

PLAYED AT BATH.

WEDNESDAY, THURSDAY & FRIDAY, JUNE 21st, 22nd & 23rd, 1939

Drawn.

SOMERSET.

First Innings.		Second Innings.	
Lee c Watt b Wright	23	c Foster b Watt ...	29
Gimblett c Harding b Wright ...	52	c Spencer b Todd ...	14
Buse c Fagg b Wright	3	c Spencer b Wright ...	0
C. J. P. Barnwell st Levett b Wright ...	4	c Fagg b Wright ...	0
H. D. Burrough b Wright	25	c Todd b Wright ...	4
R. A. Ingle b Wright	7	st Levett b Wright ...	6
Luckes c Fagg b Watt	0	c and b Wright ...	5
Andrews c Harding b Wright ...	2	c Fagg b Wright ...	2
G. M. Bennett b Wright	0	st Levett b Wright ...	9
Wellard b Watt	6	c Watt b Wright ...	48
Hazell not out	10	not out	0
Extras ...	13	Extras ...	15
Total	145	Total	129

KENT.

First Innings.		Second Innings.	
Fagg b Andrews	39	lbw b Wellard ...	6
G. H. Chalk c Wellard b Andrews ...	23	c Buse b Wellard ...	3
P. G. Foster c Gimblett b Andrews ...	1	b Andrews ...	29
B. H. Valentine b Andrews	4	c Luckes b Andrews ...	4
Todd lbw b Andrews	15	not out ...	8
Spencer c Wellard b Buse	33	b Wellard ...	0
Wright c Gimblett b Andrews ...	7	not out ...	4
Harding c Bennett b Andrews ...	12	run out ...	4
W. H. V. Levett b Buse	23		
Watt not out	11	c Lee b Andrews ...	10
Lewis c Gimblett b Buse	0		
Extras ...	8	Extras ...	4
Total	176	Total (7 wickets)	72

Bowling Analysis.

SOMERSET	First Innings.					Second Innings.			
	O.	M.	R.	W.		O.	M.	R.	W.
Todd ...	10.	2	30	—	...	10	1	31	1
Harding ...	4	—	22	—	. ...	3	—	10	—
Watt ...	11.6	—	45	2	...	11	1	28	1
Wright ...	11	3	35	8	...	17.4	6	45	8

KENT	First Innings.					Second Innings.			
	O.	M.	R.	W.		O.	M.	R.	W.
Wellard ...	22	3	53	—	...	8	1	32	3
Andrews ...	31	7	56	7	...	8	1	36	3
Buse ...	16.6	1	46	3	...				
Hazell ...	4	—	13	—	...				

Umpires: E. J. Smith and H. Cruice.

WORCESTERSHIRE

8, 10, 11 July 1939 at Kidderminster

This must be real contender for the most exciting match of the 1930s played at Kidderminster, although rain prevented any play on the first day. It was not until the last over of extra time that a result was obtained and even then it did not separate the two teams – for the first time since 1926, the match ended in a tie.

Somerset had a Mr S. Weaver in their side as an opening fast left-arm bowler, although he was much better known as Sam Weaver of Newcastle United, Chelsea and England fame. He was also the first long-throw specialist of a soccer ball. However, his bowling was indifferent and when 3 overs yielded just 16 runs he was left to show his skills as a fielder.

Fortunately, Wellard was able to take full advantage of a rain-affected wicket when he reverted to his off-breaks, taking 6 for 15. Having taken 1 for 30 in his quicker style, he finished with 7 for 45 against a batting side that relied almost entirely on the opening batsman, E. Cooper, whose determined innings of 69 represented more than half of the Worcestershire total. The last 7 wickets fell for only 18 runs leaving them 130 all out.

Whilst 130 appeared to be rather on the low side, Somerset were soon in trouble. Openers Lee (5) and Gimblett (0) were soon out, leaving Buse to come to the rescue once again and to play one of his 'special' innings; while he was only to make 26, they were 26 invaluable runs and helped Somerset to a 1-run lead on their first innings. Weaver, not noted for his batting, contributed 19 and Hazell was 13* when the last wicket fell.

What would happen second time around? Howorth and Cooper, never comfortable, again scored vital runs, but the pattern was very similar to the first innings. After their dismissal, both to Buse, Hazell came into his own and in 47 balls he demolished the remaining batsmen, taking 5 wickets for only 6 runs. A final total of 142 left the visitors needing 142 for victory.

Time now became a factor and a frantic start saw wickets fall and no batsman able to take charge. Extra time was part of the rulings in the 1930s and with 6 runs still needed for victory and the last pair, Weaver and Hazell, at the wicket, it was still anybody's game. It was not until the 4th ball of the last over that Hazell succumbed to the bowling of Howorth when the scores were level and this incredible match finally came to an end.

Horace Hazell.

Frank Lee.

SOMERSET v. WORCESTERSHIRE.

PLAYED AT KIDDERMINSTER.

SATURDAY, MONDAY & TUESDAY, JULY 8th, 10th & 11th, 1939.

A Tie.

WORCESTERSHIRE.

First Innings.		Second Innings.	
Cooper lbw b Wellard ...	69	c Hazell b Buse ...	21
Howorth c Luckes b Wellard ...	16	b Buse	45
King c Weaver b Buse ...	3	lbw b Buse ...	17
Gibbons c Priddy b Hazell	29	b Wellard ...	0
Martin b Wellard	0	c Bennett b Hazell...	25
C. H. Palmer b Wellard ...	2	c and b Hazell ...	11
J. Stanning c Priddy b Wellard	4	b Hazell ...	0
Hon. C. J. Lyttleton c Lee b Wellard ...	1	c Gimblett b Hazell...	0
E. H. Perry st Lee b Wellard ...	0	run out	1
Jenkins not out	1	not out	0
Perks c Lee b Hazell ...	0	c Gimblett b Hazell...	16
Extras ...	5	Extras ...	6
Total	130	Total	142

SOMERSET.

First Innings.		Second Innings.	
Lee b Perks	5	c Jenkins b Howorth	23
Gimblett b Perks ...	0	b Perry ...	5
Buse c King b Martin ...	26	b Perks ...	11
F. M. McRae c King b Perry ...	1	st King b Jenkins ...	28
E. F. Longrigg c Howorth b Martin ...	13	c and b Howorth ...	1
J. Priddy c Perks b Palmer ...	15	b Jenkins ...	13
Luckes b Perks	24	c Perks b Howorth ...	22
G. M. Bennett b Perry ...	10	c Martin b Perks ...	16
Wellard b Perks	0	b Perry ...	12
S. Weaver b Jenkins ...	19	not out ...	3
Hazell not out	13	b Howorth ...	4
Extras ...	5	Extras ...	3
Total	131	Total	141

Bowling Analysis.

WORCESTER	First Innings.					Second Innings.			
	O.	M.	R.	W.		O.	M.	R.	W.
Wellard ...	16	1	45	7	...	16	1	62	1
S. Weaver ...	3	—	16	—	...	1	—	13	—
Buse ...	10	2	24	1	...	21	5	55	3
Hazell ...	11.7	2	40	2	...	5.7	1	6	5

SOMERSET	First Innings.					Second Innings.			
	O.	M.	R.	W.		O.	M.	R.	W.
Perks ...	13	1	40	4	...	10	2	34	2
E. H. Perry ...	12	2	31	2	...	10	1	43	2
Martin ...	11	1	26	2	...	—	—	—	—
Howorth ..	4	1	18	—	...	9.4	1	27	4
C. H. Palmer ...	1	—	6	1	...	—	—	—	—
Jenkins ...	2.5	—	5	1	...	10	1	34	2

Perks 3 n.b.

Umpires: E. Cooke and J. Smart.

GLAMORGAN
15, 17, 18 June 1946 at Pontypridd

This was a game that ruffled the feathers of the 'powers that be' back in headquarters by what was termed to be a freak declaration. It was the only game to be played at Pontypridd during this first post-war season, and it suffered from a typically wet spell of Welsh weather. Play was stopped after lunch on the first day and a downpour on Sunday was followed by even wetter weather on Monday, giving little hope of any further play. The two captains, the very experienced John Clay of Glamorgan and the part-time amateur John Barnwell of Somerset, agreed to give the spectators their first opportunity of watching post-war cricket by agreeing to contrive a finish.

John Barnwell declared the Somerset innings at Saturday's score of 51 for 1 on the understanding that Glamorgan's innings would close at the same score. Their 51 runs were scored off just 28 balls by two 'non-bowlers', Frank Lee and Trevor Jones, which left as much time as possible for the 'arranged' game.

There remained 270 minutes in which to play what was in effect a one-innings match giving at the same time entertainment to a surprisingly large crowd. Looking back, it was obvious that Glamorgan held all the trump cards – the experienced Johnny Clay had manoeuvred them into a position where a victory was possible and a defeat unlikely.

Somerset's innings was a complete disaster, as they failed to combat the excellent bowling of A.D.G. Matthews, who took 7 wickets for only 12 runs off 17 overs. With Judge taking 3 for 35, they were lucky to total 53 (of which the two openers, Frank Lee and Harold Gimblett, contributed 29 and 12 respectively). Four consecutive 0's followed and the innings lasted 33.5 overs. The drying pitch was almost unplayable once the effects of the roller had worn off.

The only thing that could spare John Barnwell's blushes was further rain and he was almost saved, but Glamorgan were not to be denied, winning easily by 8 wickets and scoring their runs off 28 overs.

62 overs had been bowled and at least the loyal Welsh supporters had seen their side win a match that was to be deemed unfair to other Counties as it gave them 12 points that they would have been most unlikely to have obtained under normal conditions. At least it gave the 'rules' committee something to do back at Lord's.

John Barnwell.

J.C. Clay.

SOMERSET v. GLAMORGAN

PLAYED AT PONTYPRIDD
SATURDAY, MONDAY and TUESDAY, JUNE 15th, 17th and 18th, 1946

Somerset lost by 8 wickets

SOMERSET

First Innings.		Second Innings.	
F. S. Lee c Wooller b Judge 15		c Wooller b Matthews ...	29
H. Gimblett not out 26		c Judge b Matthews ...	12
J. Lawrence not out 4		b Matthews	0
C. J. P. Barnwell did not bat		c Dyson b Matthews ...	0
H. T. Buse ,,		c Clay b Matthews ...	0
J. W. Seamer ,,		c Wooller b Judge ...	0
A. T. M. Jones ,,		c Watkins b Matthews ...	0
W. H. Andrews ,,		b Judge	5
A. W. Wellard ,,		b Matthews	3
W. T. Luckes ,,		not out	0
H. L. Hazell ,,		b Judge	0
Extras ... 6		Extras ... 4

*Total (1 wicket) 51
*Innings declared closed

Total 53

GLAMORGAN

First Innings.		Second Innings.	
W. E. Jones not out 40		lbw b Wellard	5
W. Watkins c Seamer b Jones 3			
G. Lavis not out 8			
A. Dyson did not bat		b. Buse	18
E. Davies ,,		not out	21
W. Wooller ,,		not out	0
H. Davies ,,			
P. F. Judge ,,			
A. Matthews ,,			
J. C. Clay ,,			
Extras ... 00		Extras ... 10

*Total (1 wicket) 51
*Innings declared closed

Total (2 wickets) 54

Bowling Analysis

SOMERSET	First Innings.					Second Innings.			
	O	M	R	W		O	M	R	W
Matthews ...	13.2	8	14	0	...	17	9	12	7
Judge	10	3	14	1	...	13.5	1	35	3
Wooller ...	3	0	17	0	...				
Clay					...	3	1	2	0

GLAMORGAN	First Innings.					Second Innings.			
	O	M	R	W		O	M	R	W
Lee	3.4	0	30	0	...				
Jones ...	3	0	21	1					
Wellard ...					...	14	4	22	1
Andrews ...					...	8	3	11	0
Buse					...	6	1	9	1
Hazell ...					...	0.2	0	2	0

Umpires : Coleman and Cruice.

THE INDIANS
31 July, 1, 2 August 1946 at Taunton

The return of first-class cricket after the war was rewarded by huge crowds, and it was a near record crowd at Taunton when India became the first post-war touring team to visit England.

Though the weather had been unkind to the tourists, they had plundered runs from most County attacks. Merchant and the captain, Nawab of Pataudi (reported in one paper as Pat O'Day!), were the star attractions showing their undoubted talents and experience, but it was not to be their day against a spirited Somerset attack.

Conditions suited both Andrews and Buse, Merchant was soon removed for 0 by a beautiful ball from Andrews. Playing in borrowed boots – his own had fallen to pieces and he maintained that he could not afford a new pair – Andrews continued to torment the Indians and by lunchtime they were all out for only 64. This was to be their lowest score of their tour.

Andrews and Buse shared the wickets and whilst Somerset supporters were delighted with their efforts, they were also fearful of what might be in store for their own batsmen. Any doubts were soon forgotten as Gimblett and Frank Lee put on 182 for the first wicket before Lee was run out.

Mickey Walford, making his debut for Somerset, more than lived up to his reputation and scored a superb 140* with classic shots all around the wicket. At last Somerset had got an amateur of real class, though sadly only for the holiday periods.

A score of over 500 was indeed rare against a touring side, but it was achieved and though India fought back with Pataudi and Merchant thrilling the large crowd with their delightful batting, they were unable to score enough runs to make Somerset bat a second time and lost by an innings and 11 runs.

The county ground at Taunton.

H. Gimblett.

M.M. Walford.

Bertie Buse.

E.F. Longrigg.

The Indian touring team, 1946. From left to right, back row: P. Gupta MBE (manager), V.S. Hazare, V. Mankad, Abdul Hafeez, R.S. Modi, S.W. Sohoni, R.B. Nimbalkar, S.G. Shinde, W. Ferguson (scorer). Middle row: S. Banerjee, Mushtaq Ali, V.M. Merchant, Nawab of Pataudi, L. Amarnath, D.D. Hindlekar, C.S. Nayudu. Front row: Gul Mohamed, C.T. Sarwate.

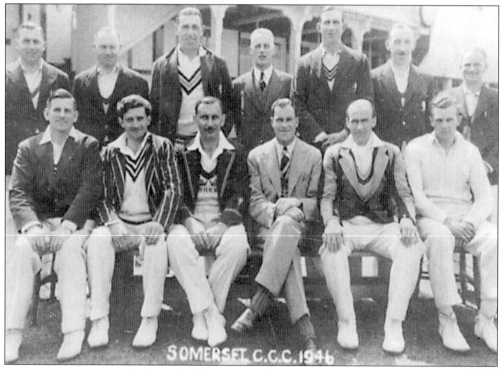

A Somerset XI, 1946. From left to right, back row: H. Gimblett, F.S. Lee, A.W. Wellard, R.F. Trump (scorer), W.H.R. Andrews, H.F.T. Buse, J. Lawrence. Front row: W.T. Luckes, A.T.M. Jones, N.S. Mitchell-Innes, E.F. Longrigg, C.J.P. Barnwell, G.R. Langdale.

SOMERSET v. INDIA

PLAYED AT TAUNTON
WEDNESDAY, THURSDAY and FRIDAY, JULY 31st, AUGUST 1st and 2nd, 1946

Somerset won by an innings and 11 runs

INDIA

First Innings.		Second Innings.	
V. M. Merchant c Luckes b Andrews ...	0	c Hazell b Buse ...	87
S. Mushtaq Ali b Andrews	20	run out	1
Nawab of Pataudi c Walford b Buse ...	29	c Luckes b Meyer ...	76
L. Amarnath c Lawrence b Buse	1	c Longrigg b Hazell ...	41
A. Hafeez b Andrews	0	c Buse b Andrews ...	38
V. S. Hazare c Hazell b Buse	0	c Gimblett b Hazell ...	43
Gul Mohomed c Walford b Buse	2	lbw b Buse	0
V. Mankad b Buse	4	b Lawrence	8
S. W. Sohoni c Longrigg b Andrews ...	3	st. Luckes b Lawrence ...	32
C. T. Sarwate not out	0	not out	66
D. D. Hindlekar c Walford b Andrews ...	4	st Luckes b Buse ...	30
Extras ...	1	Extras ...	9
Total 64		**Total 431**	

SOMERSET
First Innings.

F. S. Lee run out	76
H. Gimblett c Merchant b Mankad ...	102
R. J. O. Meyer c Mushtaq Ali b Mankad ...	19
F. Castle b Sarwate	0
E. F. Longrigg c Pataudi b Mankad ...	74
J. Lawrence b Sarwate	5
M. M. Walford not out	141
H. T. Buse not out	59
W. T. Luckes, W. H. Andrews and H. Hazell did not bat	
Extras ...	30
*Total (6 wickets) 506	

*Innings declared closed.

Bowling Analysis

INDIA		First Innings.					Second Innings.		
		O	M	R	W		O	M	R	W
Andrews	...	19	5	36	5	...	27	2	94	1
Buse ...	...	18	6	27	5	...	32.3	5	108	3
Meyer ...	...						29	6	72	1
Lawrence	...					...	20	3	83	2
Hazell ...	...					...	17	3	52	2
Gimblett	...					...	1	0	13	0

Andrews 1 n b   Meyer 1 n b

SOMERSET		First Inning.			
		O	M	R	W
Amarnath	...	48	17	87	0
Sohoni	...	31	7	119	0
Mankad	...	50	10	136	3
Hazare	...	15	4	32	0
Sarwate	...	39	8	95	2
Pataudi	...	1	0	7	0

Sohoni 2 n b

Umpires : Cooke and Cruice.

MIDDLESEX

10, 12, 13 May 1947 at Lord's

In a comparatively low-scoring match, Somerset were successful by just one wicket after all had appeared to be lost.

Bill Edrich, a 'new' amateur after many years as a professional, showed that his change in status had not affected his batting skills and later in the game he was to show that his bowling skills could even have increased. He scored a very fine 102 out of a Middlesex total of 231 before finally falling to Buse, who had the magnificent figures of 6 for 52. The match also marked the occasion when a new name appeared on the Somerset scoreboard – one that would remain for many years, Tremlett.

Somerset faired badly and were bowled out for 134, with that man Edrich taking 4 wickets for 5 runs in only 24 balls and finishing with 4 for 46. When Middlesex batted again, new boy Maurice Tremlett did even better, taking 5 wickets in 5 overs at a cost of only 8 runs. Veteran Arthur Wellard helped to remove other batsmen and Middlesex tottered to 78 all out.

Could Somerset score 176 to win? By close of play on the second day, they were 101 for 5 with all the recognised batsmen back in the pavilion. On the final day, 75 runs were required to win, with 5 wickets in hand, but with the pitch deteriorating and rain in the air, even this was far from encouraging, but Luckes and Hill added an invaluable 38. They were both out, leaving Tremlett and Hazell to attempt an improbable victory. They saw Somerset through to lunch and were then within 16 runs of their target.

Did they eat any lunch? Did they discuss tactics? On returning to the wicket they both played defensively, taking singles whenever possible, until Tremlett hit a magnificent straight drive for 6 and was soon to finish the match, ending with 19* – what a debut!

Middlesex were very generous in defeat, applauding the batsmen from the field as they left for the pavilion, and England hoped that they had found a new fast bowler who was also a useful batsman. This was a rare but well deserved victory for Somerset.

Maurice Tremlett.

Bill Edrich.

SOMERSET v. MIDDLESEX

PLAYED AT LORDS

SATURDAY, MONDAY and TUESDAY, MAY 10th, 12th and 13th, 1947

Somerset won by one wicket

MIDDLESEX

First Innings.		Second Innings.	
J. D. Robertson b Tremlett	39	b Buse	30
S. M. Brown lbw b Wellard	7	b Wellard	0
W. J. Edrich c Luckes b Buse	102	c Lawrence b Wellard	3
D. Compton c Woodhouse b Buse	6	b Tremlett	25
J. Eaglestone b Buse	0	c Lawrence b Tremlett	4
F. G. Mann b Buse	27	b Tremlett ...	0
A. Thompson c Wellard b Tremlett	5	b Tremlett ...	0
L. Compton b. Tremlett	11	b Tremlett ...	0
J. Sims c and b Buse	3	not out	6
J. Young not out	6	c Luckes b Wellard ...	1
L. Gray c Hazell b Buse	5	run out	4
Extras	20	Extras ...	5
Total	231	Total	78

SOMERSET

First Innings.		Second Innings.	
F. S. Lee c D. Compton b Young	28	c Robertson b Young	38
H. Gimblett b Edrich	25	b Edrich	13
H. T. Buse lbw b Gray...	1	c L. Compton b Gray	3
G. E. S. Woodhouse b Edrich	7	b Edrich	21
R. J. O. Meyer c Robertson b Sims	1	b Gray	4
J. Lawrence c Mann b Sims	30	b Young	19
E. Hill b Edrich	0	c Edrich b Young ...	17
W. T. Luckes c Edrich b Gray	9	c L. Compton b Gray	26
A. W. Wellard b Edrich	17	b Edrich	5
M. F. Tremlett c Gray b Sims	5	not out	19
H. L. Hazell not out	0	not out	8
Extras	11	Extras ...	5
Total	134	Total (for 9 wkts.)	178

Bowling Analysis

MIDDLESEX	First Innings.				Second Innings.			
	O	M	R	W	O	M	R	W
Buse ...	23	8	52	6	4	2	14	1
Wellard ...	22	4	49	1	16.3	7	20	3
Tremlett ...	24	5	47	3	14	3	39	5
Hazell ...	4	0	13	0				
Lawrence ...	12	2	40	0				
Meyer ...	4	1	10	0				

SOMERSET	First Innings.				Second Innings.			
	O	M	R	W	O	M	R	W
Gray ...	24	10	25	2	29.2	7	51	3
Edrich ...	16	3	46	4	22	8	47	3
Young ...	11	6	12	1	34	14	48	3
Sims ...	15.4	4	40	3	7	0	27	0

Sims 1 wide

Umpires : Coleman and Hills.

GLOUCESTERSHIRE

2, 3, 4 August 1947 at Bristol

The summer of 1947 will long be remembered by cricket lovers as the longest (and hottest) summer of the twentieth century. The August Bank Holiday fixture between the two West Country rivals only lasted two days, and many were perhaps happy to escape the heat and move to the beach on what should have been the last.

Gloucestershire, batting first, lost their two star batsmen, Barnett and Allen, before Neale and Wilson ensured that they reached 244. Somerset used 7 bowlers with R.J.O. Meyer taking the last two wickets for 7 runs off 8.3 overs. In all 104.3 overs were bowled and of the 244 runs scored, some 35 were extras – not a very exciting Bank Holiday!

Somerset never looked like reaching a reasonable score, particularly when Goddard replaced Lambert after the latter had bowled just one over. Though expensive (67 runs from 10 overs), he proceeded to take 7 wickets and with Barnett keeping the other end quiet, it was touch and go whether the follow-on would be averted. A final total of 98 was achieved thanks to 18 from Wellard after Lawrence had hit a six and 5 fours in an all-out attack on Goddard.

A very large Bank Holiday crowd saw Gloucestershire bat again and they found spin bowling the order of the day. Hazell tied up one end with only 62 runs coming from 23 overs, which included 5 wickets, and once again it was Neale and Wilson that enabled Gloucestershire to declare at 195 for 9 leaving Somerset the unlikely target of 324 to win.

Disaster struck at once. Walford 5, Coope 1, Lawrence 0 gave Barnett and Lambert two wickets each before Goddard had even turned an arm. However, he only needed 3 overs to finish off the innings, taking 5 wickets in 7 balls at a cost of only 4 runs. His 'hat-trick' of Wellard, Meyer and Hazell saw Somerset all out for 25 – a defeat by 300 runs.

On a spinner's paradise, Sam Cook only bowled 10 balls, taking 1 wicket for 1 run before returning to Painswick and his garden!

Somerset CCC, 1947. From left to right, back row: J. Lawrence, M. Coope, W. Andrews, R. Trump (scorer), M. Tremlett, A. Vickery, H. Hazell. Front row: H. Gimblett, A. Wellard, R.J.O. Meyer, W.T. Luckes, H.T.F. Buse.

SATURDAY, MONDAY and TUESDAY, AUGUST 2nd, 4th and 5th, 1947

Somerset lost by 316 runs

GLOUCESTERSHIRE

First Innings.		Second Innings.	
C. J. Barnett lbw b Wellard	16	c Meyer b Hazell ...	11
B. O. Allen b Tremlett	10	st. Lee b Wellard ...	2
W. L. Neale lbw b Langdale	63	lbw b Hazell ...	45
J. F. Crapp lbw b Langdale	13	lbw b Hazell ...	26
G. M. Emmett c Watts b Hazell ...	1	b Hazell ...	39
G. W. Parker c Lawrence b Hazell ...	18	b Wellard ...	6
A. E. Wilson b Meyer	61	b Hazell ...	27
G. Lambert b Langdale	0	run out	12
C. J. Scott c Watts b Hazell	22	c Buse b Meyer ...	1
T. W. Goddard lbw b Meyer	5	not out	1
C. Cook not out	0		
Extras ...	35	Extras ...	25
Total	244	Total (9 wkts. dec.)	195

SOMERSET

First Innings.		Second Innings.	
M. M. Walford st. Wilson b Goddard ...	10	b Lambert	5
R. J. O. Meyer b Goddard	3	lbw b Goddard	0
H. E. Watts c Scott b Goddard ...	4	lbw b Barnett ...	0
J. Lawrence c Scott b Goddard ...	34	c Neale b Barnett ...	0
F. S. Lee b Goddard	10	b Goddard ...	17
G. R. Langdale b Barnett	0	b Goddard ...	0
M. Coope c Allen b Barnett ...	11	b Lambert ...	1
M. F. Tremlett st. Wilson b Barnett ...	1	c Emmett b Goddard ...	1
H. T. Buse lbw b Goddard	0	not out ...	1
A. W. Wellard c Scott b Goddard ...	18	c Parker b Goddard ...	0
H. L. Hazell not out	3	lbw b Cook	0
Extras ...	4	Extras ...	0
Total	98	Total	25

Bowling Analysis

GLOUCESTERSHIRE	First Innings.					Second Innings.			
	O	M	R	W		O	M	R	W
Buse ...	8	2	24	0					
Wellard ...	20	5	54	1	...	15	3	36	2
Hazell ...	27	13	35	3	...	23.2	5	62	5
Tremlett ...	13	2	27	1	...	4	2	8	0
Langdale ...	17	5	31	3	...	7	1	16	0
Lawrence ...	9	1	31	0					
Meyer ...	8.3	5	7	2	...	12	2	48	1

Langdale 1 wide.

SOMERSET	First Innings.					Second Innings.			
	O	M	R	W		O	M	R	W
Barnett ...	12	4	24	3	...	5	2	10	2
Lambert ...	1	0	9	0	...	3	1	10	2
Goddard ...	10.4	1	61	7	...	3	1	4	5
Cook ...						1.4	1	1	1

Umpires: Mitchison and Heaton

SUSSEX

18, 19, 20 August 1948 at Eastbourne

A large mid-week holiday crowd enjoying perfect weather were rewarded by runs from both sides and a particularly fine innings from Harold Gimblett, who was to become the first post-war batsman to score 300.

Many supporters felt that Gimblett had been unlucky not to be selected for the fifth and final Test against the Australians which had finished the previous day and no doubt the selectors were embarrassed when this game came to an end.

Sussex, batting first, took their time in recording a formidable total of 434 for 9 before declaring. The Langridge brothers did the bulk of the scoring, John with 78 and James with a typical workmanlike 100, but better fare was still to come.

Gimblett, opening with schoolmaster M.M. Walford, took full advantage of an easy paced pitch and started their innings after lunch on the second day thrilled the holiday crowd in putting on 180 before Walford fell to Wood. Four quick wickets did not deter him from continuing his assault on the Sussex bowlers and with Coope added 210 in 150 minutes, of which the latter scored 89.

Playing every shot in the book against eight Sussex bowlers, he batted for just over seven and a half hours, giving two very difficult chances before he was finally defeated by George Cox. Incredibly, he cleared the boundary on only two occasions, though 37 other balls were despatched to the boundary and his final score of 310 remained a record until it was beaten by Viv Richards against Warwickshire,

As a match it had petered out by the end of the second day, but the crowd returned to the feast and saw Somerset reach 584 for 8 before declaring and having to be satisfied with first-innings points.

There was time for 20 overs of all sorts to be bowled. Gimblett was not too tired to bowl for 4 of them and it gave the opportunity for the captain, George Woodhouse, to take his only wicket in first-class cricket when he had Billy Griffith caught by Arthur Wellard.

Harold Gimblett's 310.

SOMERSET v. SUSSEX

PLAYED AT EASTBOURNE
WEDNESDAY, THURSDAY AND FRIDAY, AUGUST 18TH, 19TH AND 20TH, 1948.

Drawn game.

SUSSEX

First Innings.		Second Innings.	
John Langridge, b Tremlett	78		
H. W. Parks, c Woodhouse, b Hazell	46		
G. H. G. Doggart, c Luckes, b Wellard	32	c Wellard, b Coope	21
C. Oakes, c Walford, b Hazell	58		
James Langridge, c Tremlett, b Hazell	100		
G. Cox, b Hazell	28	not out	14
P. D. S. Blake, b Wellard	16	not out	42
H. T. Bartlett, not out	18		
S. C. Griffith, c Luckes, b Hazell	36	c Wellard, b Woodhouse	1
J. Wood, c Luckes, b Buse	5		
J. Cornford, not out	1		
B 11, lb 5	16	W 1	1
Total	*434	Total for 2 wickets	79

*Innings declared closed.

SOMERSET
First Innings.

H. Gimblett, c Wood, b Cox	310
M. M. Walford, c Jn. Langridge, b Wood	71
H. E. Watts, b Cornford	11
H. T. Buse, c Griffith, b Jas. Langridge	7
G. E. S. Woodhouse, b Doggart	19
M. Coope, b Jas. Langridge	89
M. F. Tremlett, run out	29
J. Lawrence, not out	0
A. W. Wellard, c Parks, b Cox	24
W. T. Luckes, did not bat.	
H. L. Hazell, " "	
B 12, lb 11, w 1	24
Total	*584

*Innings declared closed.

BOWLING ANALYSIS.

SUSSEX	First Innings.				Second Innings.			
	O.	M.	R.	W.	O.	M.	R.	W.
Wellard	31	4	109	2				
Tremlett	28	4	89	1				
Buse	28	7	65	1				
Lawrence	26	5	73	0				
Hazell	29	6	82	5				
Gimblett					4	0	18	0
G. E. S. Woodhouse					4	0	8	1
Coope					6	1	25	1
M. M. Walford					3	0	12	0
H. E. Watts					3	0	15	0

Walford 1 wide.

SOMERSET	First Innings.			
	O.	M.	R.	W.
Wood	37	11	104	1
Cornford	32	10	75	1
Cox	15	2	46	2
Oakes	31	3	121	0
Jas. Langridge	50	10	136	2
John Langridge	8	1	26	0
Bartlett	2	0	12	0
Doggart	8	1	40	1

Doggart 1 wide.

Umpires : D. Hendren and P. Mills.

LANCASHIRE

6, 8, 9 June 1953 at Bath

The long-serving, long-suffering Bertie Buse was granted a benefit some 24 years after playing his first game for Somerset. The thought of playing in front of his local supporters prompted him to select the opening game of the Bath festival against Lancashire for his 'big day'. Dubbed 'the butler' by John Arlott due to his rather odd approach to the wicket whilst bowling coupled with a batting style that defied description, he was a much respected performer with both bat and ball and everyone hoped that he would have a successful and profitable benefit. Arnold Ridley, author of *The Ghost Train* but probably better known as Godfrey in *Dad's Army*, wished him well with three fine days plus lots of runs, wickets and money, but it was not to be.

Bertie, as the beneficiary, tossed up and on being successful decided to bat. In under an hour and a half Somerset were dismissed for just 55 on a wicket that was certainly unpredictable, though the rot started with Harold Gimblett being run out before he had scored a run. No Somerset batsman reached double figures and Bertie was almost proud of his contribution – 5 runs. Brian Langford, making his debut, earned praise for his 7*, but must have wondered whether a career in county cricket was a wise choice.

Lancashire, batting before lunch, had six current or future Test players in their side, but Bertie was soon amongst the wickets, taking the first 4 for only 16 runs. Peter Marner was to take 18 from one of his overs but Lancashire could only manage 158 with Bertie ending up with 6 for 41.

There were still two and a half hours left when Somerset began their second innings, but they were not able to stretch the game into the second day, as they were dismissed for a miserable 79, of which the last pair scored 35 in 20 minutes – a defeat by an innings and 24 runs in less than a day.

It was a day to remember, although one that Bertie would perhaps have liked to forget. After all expenses the benefit fund showed a very small profit though Somerset later decided to meet the match costs which was much appreciated by the beneficiary.

Bertie Buse.

SOMERSET v. LANCASHIRE

PLAYED AT BATH.
JUNE 6th. 8th and 9th, 1953

Lost by an Innings and 24 Runs.

SOMERSET.

First Innings.		Second Innings.	
Gimblett, H., run out	0	c Wharton, b Tattersall	5
Lawrence, J., c Ikin, b Tattersall	8	c Wharton, b Statham	0
Smith, R., c Place, b Tattersall	9	b Statham	0
Tremlett, M. F., c Statham, b Tattersall	4	b Statham	1
Buse, H. T. F., c Grieves, b Tattersall	5	c Grieves, b Tattersall	3
Stephenson, H. W., c Marner, b Tattersall	8	b Tattersall	14
B. G. Brocklehurst, c Marner, b Hilton	2	c Hilton, b Tattersall	2
P. D. Deshon, c Edrich, b Tattersall	0	c Wharton, b Statham	9
S. S. Rogers, st. Parr, b Hilton	7	c Grieves, b Tattersall	0
J. Redman, c Place, b Tattersall	1	not out	27
Langford, B., not out	7	b Tattersall	8
b. 2, l.b. 2	4	b. 1, l.b. 9	10
Total	55	Total	79

1st Innings : 1 for 12, 2-13, 3-17, 4-22, 5-34, 6-40, 7-40, 8-47, 9-47, 10-55.
2nd Innings : 1 for 3, 2-3, 3-5, 4-7, 5-26, 6-27, 7-36, 8-37, 9-44, 10-79.

LANCASHIRE.

Washbrook, C., lbw, b Buse	20
Ikin, J., c Tremlett, b Buse	8
Place, W., lbw, b Buse	11
Edrich, G., c Brocklehurst, b Buse	2
Grieves, K., c Tremlett, b Lawrence	2
Wharton, A., b Redman	21
Marner, P., b Redman	44
Hilton, M., b Buse	19
Parr, F., not out	15
Tattersall, R., c Stephenson, b Buse	2
Statham, B., c Tremlett, b Langford	6
b. 4, l.b. 4	8
Total	158

1st Innings : 1 for 22, 2-33, 3-41, 4-44, 5-46, 6-116, 7-117, 8-140, 9-155, 10-158.

BOWLING ANALYSIS.

Somerset.

	First Innings.				Second Innings.			
	O.	M.	R.	W.	O.	M.	R.	W.
Statham	8	4	14	—	10	4	13	4
Tattersall	12.4	4	25	7	11.3	2.	44	6
Hilton	5	1	12	2	2	—	12	—

Lancashire.

	O.	M.	R.	W.
Buse	12.4	3	41	6
Redman	6	1	32	2
Smith	1	—	8	—
Langford	3	—	18	1
Lawrence	8	2	31	1
Tremlett	2	—	20	—

Umpires : E. Boulton-Carter and J. S. Buller.
Somerset won the toss.

LANCASHIRE

25, 27, 28 June 1960 at Taunton

The first day saw some beautiful batting by Peter Wight who scored a well deserved century and he almost succeeded in repeating this in the second innings, but both the spectators and Peter were more than satisfied even though he was dismissed for 90.

Somerset led the way with a first-innings total of 221, which was sufficient to gain them a lead of 21 after some indifferent batting by Lancashire. Alan Whitehead took 4 rather expensive wickets but for a time appeared to be the answer to Somerset's prayers for a slow left-arm bowler. Tight bowling at the other end by Bill Alley was rewarded by 4 wickets at a cost of 45 and Somerset on batting a second time scored 301 to leave Lancashire 322 to get in 265 minutes. Colin McCool scored exactly 100 in a fine innings and with Peter Wight scored 70 per cent of Somerset's runs.

Without Bill Alley, who was injured, Somerset faced a hard task in dismissing Lancashire in what time was left, though Ken Biddulph helped by getting a quick wicket. Wharton and Dyson scored rapidly and a rare Chris Greetham wicket was a bonus when he clean bowled Dyson for 47. Australian and hard-hitting Ken Grieves, who was in fine form, posed the next threat and the rate of scoring remained too high for Somerset's comfort. However, whilst the runs still came wickets began to fall and it was obvious that nothing short of victory was in Lancashire's mind, even though they were short of experienced batsmen further down the order.

Tension ran high as the minutes ticked by and with 45 minutes left, only 47 runs were required for a Lancashire victory, but there was only one wicket remaining. Ken Higgs and Roy Tattersall were Test players, but were better known for their bowling rather than their batting. However, with only 12 minutes left, they had fought their way to within 8 runs when a loud and long appeal by Ken Biddulph for lbw against Roy Tattersall was upheld and Somerset had won a famous victory over the Red Rose County.

Peter Wight.

Colin McCool.

SOMERSET v. LANCASHIRE, at Taunton. 25th, 27th and 28th June, 1960

Won by 8 Runs—14 Points

SOMERSET

G. Atkinson b Dyson	27	lbw b Greenhough	29
R. Virgin b Higgs	3	lbw b Greenhough	8
P. B. Wight c Booth b Dyson	100	c Clayton b Marner	90
C. L. McCool c Grieves b Dyson	20	b Higgs	100
C. Greetham b Dyson	12	c Clayton b Higgs	8
W. E. Alley c Grieves b Dyson	12	retired hurt	2
B. A. Langford c Tattersall b Greenhough	3	b Higgs	24
H. W. Stephenson c Dyson b Greenhough	19	lbw b Greenhough	34
F. Herting not out	16	b Higgs	0
A. Whitehead lbw b Dyson	0	not out	2
K. Biddulph st Clayton b Dyson	6	c Clayton b Greenhough	2
lb 3	3	lb 2	2

Runs per Over 2·35   **Total 221**   **Total 301**

	O	M	R	W		O	M	R	W
Higgs	12	3	39	1		23	5	51	4
Marner	5	2	9	—		9	2	22	1
Tattersall	17	6	21	—		12	4	41	—
Greenhough	28	8	59	2		28	6	79	4
Dyson	24·5	4	83	7		8	—	42	—
Barber	7	3	7	—		12	2	47	—
Booth						4	—	17	—

LANCASHIRE

A. Wharton c Stephenson b Alley	24	b Langford	81
B. Booth c McCool b Alley	15	lbw b Biddulph	0
J. Dyson not out	66	b Greetham	47
K. Grieves c Whitehead b Alley	21	c Biddulph b Whitehead	39
P. Marner c Virgin b Whitehead	42	c Herting b Biddulph	12
R. W. Barber c Alley b Whitehead	9	c McCool b Langford	11
A. Bolton c Alley b Whitehead	2	c Langford b Whitehead	44
G. Clayton c McCool b Whitehead	0	b McCool	30
T. Greenhough b Langford	0	st Stephenson b McCool	4
K. Higgs c Atkinson b Alley	5	not out	23
R. Tattersall c McCool b Biddulph	8	lbw b Biddulph	14
b 4, lb 3, w 1	8	b 5, lb 3, w 1	9

Runs per Over 2·35   **Total 200**   **Total 314**

	O	M	R	W		O	M	R	W
Biddulph	13·1	4	34	1		17·3	5	39	3
Herting	4	—	16	—		14	1	67	—
Alley	24	6	45	4		23	7	72	2
Langford	27	16	35	1		23	7	72	2
McCool	8	3	15	—		5	—	28	2
Whitehead	9	2	47	4		13	—	54	2
Greetham						12	1	45	1

McCool 1 w   McCool 1 w

Cambridge University

29, 30 June, 1 July 1960 at Taunton

Can it be, after all, that truth is stranger than fiction? A game of cricket that produced 1,365 runs on a perfect Taunton wicket broke numerous records, but was enjoyed by a relatively small crowd on all three days.

Somerset batted first against a good Cambridge side which included a number of players who would go on to represent England at Test level. An opening partnership between Roy Virgin and Graham Atkinson set the tone for the rest of the match. 172 runs had been scored before the first wicket fell, and each went on to record a century, Peter Wight batting at number three was not to be overshadowed and likewise scored a century – and this was only the first day. Somerset had the luxury of declaring at 418 for 7, but the University were not daunted by this mountain of runs.

An opening partnership that was even better than that of Somerset saw 198 runs on the board and again both openers, Roger Prideaux and Tony Lewis, went on to record centuries. Once again number three, M.J.L. Willard followed suit with 101* when the Cambridge captain, Chris Harman, with 416 for 4 showing on the scoreboard, also declared shortly after play started on the third day.

Quick runs by Somerset saw Peter Wight fail by just one run to record a second century and the captain, Harold Stephenson, thought it was safe to leave the University to attempt to score 266 in 175 minutes. How wrong can a captain be? Roger Prideaux scored his second century, Tony Lewis 71 and an opening partnership of 137 was scored in just 81 minutes. In the final over of the match, J.R. Barnard hit a glorious cover drive to the boundary and a magnificent feast of runs came to an end.

Cricket history was made in this match as all four opening batsmen reached three figures:

      Atkinson and Virgin   172 and 112

      Prideaux and Lewis   198 and 137

Bowlers would prefer to forget this match but A. Hurd deserved credit for his 4 for 99 off 24 overs when Somerset were chasing runs in their second innings.

Somerset CCC, 1960. From left to right, back row: R. Virgin, F. Herting, K. Biddulph, T. Tout (scorer), A. Whitehead, K.E. Palmer, G. Atkinson. Front row: A.A. Baig, M.F. Tremlett, H.W. Stephenson, C.L. McCool, B.A. Langford, P.B. Wight.

A.R. Lewis.

Roger Prideaux.

Roy Virgin.

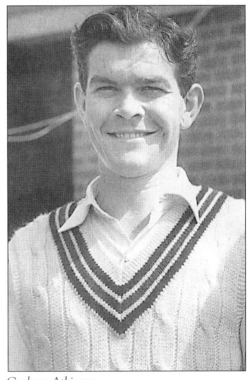

Graham Atkinson.

Peter Wight – 105 and 99.

SOMERSET v. CAMBRIDGE UNIVERSITY, at Taunton.

29th, 30th June and 1st July, 1960

Lost by 6 Wickets

SOMERSET

G. Atkinson c & b Kirby	103	c Willard b Hurd	50
R. Virgin c Lewis b Hurd	113	c Kirby b Hurd	70
P. B. Wight c Kirby b Brody	105	c Howland b Hurd	99
C. Greetham c Howland b Willard	61	c Atkins b Hurd	5
M. Kitchen c Howland b Brody	0	c Kirby b Willard	15
G. L. Keith c Prideaux b Coghlan	20		
M. Lawrence not out	6	} did not bat	
H. W. Stephenson c Howland b Coghlan	0		
F. Herting }		not out	10
H. Suily } did not bat			
E. Bryant }		} did not bat	
lb 6, w 1, nb 3	10	b 9, lb 4, w 1	14
Total for 7 wkts dec.	418	Total for 5 wkts dec.	263

	O	M	R	W		O	M	R	W
Brody	23	2	99	2					
Coghlan	14·2	2	48	2	...	13	1	38	—
Willard	19	5	58	1	...	11·5	1	66	1
Hurd	31	6	110	1	...	24	3	99	4
Kirby	14	2	60	1	...	10	1	35	—
Atkins	6	1	33	—	...	1	—	11	—

Coghlan 1 w & 2 nb, Brody 1 nb   Atkins 1 w

CAMBRIDGE UNIVERSITY

R. M. Prideaux c Atkinson b Bryant	102	c Stephenson b Greetham	106
A. R. Lewis c Wight b Herting	106	st Stephenson b Lawrence	71
M. J. L. Willard not out	101	lbw b Herting	33
D. Kirby lbw b Lawrence	12	c Stephenson b Greetham	9
N. S. K. Reddy c Atkinson b Virgin	75	not out	17
J. R. Bernard not out	15	not out	27
G. Atkins }			
C. B. Howland }			
T. B. L. Coghlan } did not bat		} did not bat	
J. B. Brody }			
A. Hurd }			
b 4, w 1	5	b 4, lb 1	5
Total for 4 wkts dec.	416	Total for 4 wkts	268

	O	M	R	W		O	M	R	W
Herting	31	7	81	1	...	17	1	82	1
Greetham	33	12	75	—	...	18·3	1	80	2
Lawrence	12	3	41	1	...	8	—	38	1
Sully	21	6	59	—	...	10	1	46	—
Bryant	41	13	107	1	...	4	—	17	—
Virgin	6	—	48	1					

Bryant 1 w

SURREY

7, 8, 9 June 1961 at Taunton

With Somerset's groundsmen producing another perfect wicket, batsmen on both sides were able to enjoy three days of stroke-making in good June weather. In all, 1,246 runs were scored with the loss of only 20 wickets with four batsmen scoring a century and one scoring a century in each innings.

Winning the toss, Peter May, absent from the England side, had no hesitation in batting, although Surrey were to lose two wickets, Stewart and Parsons, for only 73 runs. The spectators were not disappointed when England's premier batsman walked to the wicket and treated them to a majestic display with shots all around the wicket, but it was his on-driving which really gave the fielders no chance. He remained supreme until he declared at 358 for 4 with a personal tally of 153*.

Somerset started their first innings in a similar fashion, losing Graham Atkinson and Brian Roe for only 36, but then Peter Wight and Bill Alley took the Surrey attack apart and in their differing ways took the score to 333 before Peter Wight fell to a caught and bowled. Bill Alley was still in full swing and by the time the captain, Harold Stephenson, declared he was 183*. His innings had occupied 260 minutes in which he hit 2 sixes and 24 boundaries.

Good as the fare had been, it was to get even better. Tindall scored an incredible century in only 96 minutes without the aid of any 'joke' bowling, and Peter May was able to declare at 273 for 3, which left Somerset three hours in which to score 271 to win.

Again two quick wickets fell, but this did not deter the remaining batsmen. Bill Alley bettered Tindall's time for a century in 90 minutes for his second century in the match and won the match for Somerset with his 17th boundary with just 4 minutes of playing time remaining. It was a batsman's match, but credit must go to the groundsmen and to the bowlers, who never gave up the struggle. It was also memorable for being the match when Bill Alley became the first Somerset player to score two not-out centuries in a match.

Bill Alley.

SOMERSET v. SURREY, at Taunton. 7th, 8th and 9th June, 1961
Won by 4 Wickets—12 Points

SURREY

M. J. Stewart c Lomax b Biddulph	16	c Stephenson b Biddulph	24
A. B. D. Parsons c Atkinson, G. b Lomax ...	38	c Stephenson b Atkinson, C. ...	76
M. D. Willett b Biddulph	73	c Stephenson b Biddulph	21
P. B. H. May not out	153	c Atkinson, G. b Biddulph	5
B. Constable lbw b Atkinson, C.	5	c Atkinson, C. b Langford	13
R. A. E. Tindall not out	71	not out	100
R. Swetman		not out	19
G. A. R. Lock			
E. A. Bedser } did not bat			
D. Gibson		} did not bat	
P. J. Loader			
b 1, lb 1	2	b 4, lb 11	15

Runs per Over 3·51   Total for 4 wkts dec. 358   Total for 5 wkts dec. 273

	O	M	R	W		O	M	R	W
Biddulph	24	4	84	2	...	19	4	54	3
Palmer	17	4	58	—	...	13	—	35	—
Alley	12	3	50	—	...	2	1	11	—
Lomax	13	5	37	1	...	2·1	—	4	—
Atkinson, C.	22	2	68	1	...	26	4	83	1
Langford	14	2	59	—	...	21	6	71	1

SOMERSET

G. Atkinson lbw b Lock	25	lbw b Loader	7
B. Roe c Parsons b Lock	11	b Loader	42
P. B. Wight c & b Gibson	125	b Lock	25
W. E. Alley not out	183	not out	134
J. G. Lomax c Constable b Lock	3	c Stewart b Bedser	31
J. M. Lawrence not out	10	did not bat	
H. W. Stephenson lbw b Lock	0	not out	8
C. Atkinson		b Bedser	5
K. Palmer		b Gibson...	8
B. A. Langford } did not bat			
K. Biddulph		} did not bat	
lb 4	4	b 4, lb 7, w 1	12

Runs per Over 3·30   Total for 5 wkts dec. 361·   Total for 6 wkts 272

	O	M	R	W		O	M	R	W
Loader	20	5	72	—	...	11	—	48	2
Gibson	27	4	79	1	...	7·1	—	34	1
Willett	2	1	12	—					
Lock...	28	10	64	4	...	24	2	101	1
Bedser	19	3	66	—	...	16	4	65	2
Tindall	7	1	30	—	...	4	—	12	—
Constable	6	—	34	—					

Loader 1 w

THE AUSTRALIANS
29, 30, 31 May 1968 at Taunton

On a very easy paced wicket, the Australians took full advantage of the good batting conditions and scored 434 for the loss of only 3 wickets before declaring their first innings closed.

The Chappell brothers found themselves on opposite sides with Ian having by far the better of the exchanges. Opening the innings, he put on 70 with Redpath before the latter was caught at the wicket off fellow Australian, Bill Alley. Chappell went on to add a further 233 in just over 3 hours with Cowper in an innings which included 2 sixes and 18 fours.

Somerset's Palmer brothers had opened the bowling but with little success and Greg Chappell was unable to stop his brother plundering all Somerset's bowlers although they stuck to their task and it was good batting rather than poor bowling that enabled the Aussies to score 434 runs.

Somerset started their reply in fine style with Virgin and Kitchen putting together 91 in 110 minutes. Good innings by Clarkson and Greg Chappell followed but the introduction of Gleeson soon changed the game. He took 6 for 97 in spite of some very uncharacteristic fielding by the tourists, with a number of catches going to ground. Captain Brian Langford and wicketkeeper Brooks fought hard to save the follow-on and they took the score from 257 for 9 to 304 before Langford was caught at the wicket for a very good 37.

The best innings of the match was still to come. With a lead of 130, the Aussies went for quick runs and Ian Redpath delighted the crowd with a classic innings of 112. He reached his century in 84 minutes, hitting 3 sixes and 17 fours before being bowled by Langford.

The task of scoring 313 to win was always going to be too much for Somerset and with MacKenzie at his best, bowling very fast and attacking the early batsmen, they were soon 34 for 3 – all 3 wickets to MacKenzie. A needless run-out of Bill Alley did not help and they were in dire trouble at 108 for 6.

A fine rearguard action against both the clock and good bowling followed, with Peter Robinson standing firm, batting over 2 hours for 48* but with Ken Palmer unable to bat through illness, it was left to brother Roy to withstand the wiles of Gleeson. His valuable 28 helped Robinson to add 60 for the seventh wicket but he was finally stumped with just 5 minutes of playing time remaining. Wicketkeeper Dickie Brooks, who had a very good game behind the stumps, successfully resisted and though 126 short of victory, the batsmen had shown a fighting spirit that was admired by the spectators.

Peter Robinson.

Australians

I. R. Redpath c Brooks b Alley	39	— b Langford	112	
I. M. Chappell c Robinson b Langford	147			
R. M. Cowper c Langford b R. Palmer	148			
K. D. Walters not out	61	— c Brooks b Robinson	4	
R. J. Inverarity not out	33	— not out	0	
L. R. Joslin (did not bat)		— st Brooks b Langford	61	
B 4, l-b 2	6	B 3, w 2	5	

1/70 2/303 3/356   (3 wkts., dec.) 434   1/167 2/182 3/182   (3 wkts.) 182

*†B. N. Jarman, G. D. McKenzie, J. W. Gleeson, D. A. Renneberg and E. W. Freeman did not bat.

Bowling: *First Innings*—R. Palmer 21—4—89—1; K. E. Palmer 16—1—62—0; Alley 20—10—30—1; Burgess 15—1—47—0; Langford 25—4—85—1; Robinson 13—4—57—0; Chappell 10—0—58—0. *Second Innings*—R. Palmer 7—1—43—0; K. E. Palmer 1—0—14—0; Alley 6—0—34—0; Burgess 6—0—28—0; Langford 10—2—36—2; Robinson 5—2—22—1.

Somerset

R. Virgin lbw b Cowper	56	— c and b McKenzie	0	
M. Kitchen c Freeman b Gleeson	32	— b McKenzie	34	
A. Clarkson c and b Gleeson	63	— lbw b McKenzie	7	
G. S. Chappell c Inverarity b Renneberg	44	— b McKenzie	11	
W. E. Alley b Cowper	3	— run out	26	
G. Burgess hit wkt b Gleeson	20	— b Gleeson	21	
K. E. Palmer c Redpath b Gleeson	0	— absent ill	0	
P. J. Robinson c Inverarity b Gleeson	13	— not out	48	
R. Palmer lbw b Gleeson	5	— st Jarman b Gleeson	28	
*B. A. Langford c Jarman b Renneberg	37	— lbw b Renneberg	2	
†R. A. Brooks not out	14	— not out	1	
B 9, l-b 6, w 1, n-b 1	17	B 3, l-b 6	9	

1/91 2/93 3/172 4/189 5/214   304   1/0 2/18 3/34 4/63 5/96   187
6/214 7/240 8/248 9/257   6/108 7/168 8/186

Bowling: *First Innings*—McKenzie 16—2—40—0; Renneberg 15.3—3—37—2; Freeman 12—2—50—0; Gleeson 40—13—97—6; Cowper 28—12—46—2; Chappell 5—2—17—0. *Second Innings*—McKenzie 20—4—47—4; Renneberg 14—2—44—1; Freeman 5—0—17—0; Gleeson 13—7—29—2; Cowper 12—4—16—0; Chappell 10—3—15—0; Walters 5—2—10—0.

Umpires: C. S. Elliott and A. E. Fagg.

GLOUCESTERSHIRE

29, 31 May, 1 June 1976 at Taunton

Another incredible local 'derby', with Gloucestershire winning by 8 runs having had to follow on some 254 runs behind a Somerset first innings total of 333 for 7.

On a wicket that was not conducive to quick scoring, or indeed to lengthy survival, it was left to opening batsman, Brian Rose, to ensure that a reasonable total was achieved. He made a very good 104 before Close declared, leaving Gloucestershire some batting time on the first evening.

Botham was in devastating form with the ball and, ably supported by Clapp, soon had the visitors in serious trouble. Monday morning was both dank and cold but the two bowlers continued in fine form and Gloucestershire were dismissed for 79. Stovold and Shepherd were the only batsmen to reach double figures and Botham's final analysis of 6 for 25 from 16 overs with Clapp returning 3 for 18 from 13 overs were just reward for some excellent bowling.

Although it was obvious that the follow-on had to be enforced, Somerset's bowling was greatly restricted with Burgess, injured whilst batting, unable to bowl due to a strain. When Sadiq was dismissed by Jennings for only 8, Somerset thought that they were looking at an easy victory but once again Zaheer came to Gloucestershire's rescue with another majestic century – this time scoring 141 in 165 minutes – before being bowled by Close. Steady runs from Stovold, Shepherd and Shackleton saw an unlikely total of 372 before the final wicket fell.

With plenty of time remaining, Somerset required only 119 to win and when Rose and Slocombe put on 43 before being parted, it still looked certain that Somerset would canter to victory. Mike Proctor thought otherwise. Mixing his normal quick deliveries with some clever off-spin, he took over after Tony Brown had removed Slocombe, Denning and Close.

There still seemed little danger when the score reached 97 for 3, but wickets then began to fall at an alarming rate. Even Burgess, far from fit, decided to try to stop the rot but to no avail and the last wicket fell with Somerset 9 runs short of their target.

Procter's final analysis of 6 for 35 was well deserved, as indeed was the victory, although seldom has a side lost after enforcing the follow-on with a 254-run advantage.

Brian Rose.

SOMERSET v. GLOUCESTERSHIRE

Somerset

B. C. Rose c Brassington b Graveney	104	— c Shepherd b Procter	4
P. A. Slocombe lbw b Brown	36	— lbw b Brown	1
P. W. Denning b Brown	41	— c Sadiq b Brown	
*D. B. Close b Brown	0	— c Shackleton b Brown	1(
M. J. Kitchen c Davey b Graveney	69	— c Shackleton b Procter	1(
†D. J. S. Taylor not out	41	— c Sadiq b Procter	(
G. I. Burgess retired hurt	10	— not out	
I. T. Botham b Graveney	13	— b Procter	
D. Breakwell b Davey	0	— c Shepherd b Graveney	(
K. F. Jennings not out	3	— c Stovold b Procter	(
R. J. Clapp (did not bat)		— c Sadiq b Procter	1
B 5, l-b 9, n-b 2	16	B 4, l-b 5, n-b 1	1(

1/58 2/138   (7 wkts.) 333   1/43 2/47 3/73   11(
3/138 4/237 5/290 6/326 7/327   4/97 5/97 6/100 7/101
                         8/108 9/108

Bonus points—Somerset 4, Gloucestershire 3.

Bowling: *First Innings*—Davey 20—2—82—1; Shackleton 10—1—34—0;
Procter 16—5—32—0; Brown 28—8—64—3; Graveney 24—4—94—3; Sadiq
2—0—11—0. *Second Innings*—Procter 14.3—4—35—6; Davey 5—0—20—0; Brown
9—2—27—3; Graveney 14—9—18—1.

Gloucestershire

Sadiq Mohammad c Breakwell b Botham	2	— c and b Jennings	8
N. H. C. Cooper b Botham	1	— b Botham	38
Zaheer Abbas b Clapp	5	— b Close	141
M. J. Procter c Taylor b Botham	7	— c Breakwell b Close	32
†A. W. Stovold c Close b Botham	18	— b Botham	58
D. R. Shepherd b Clapp	27	— lbw b Jennings	30
*A. S. Brown lbw b Botham	0	— b Botham	4
D. A. Graveney lbw b Jennings	2	— b Botham	0
J. H. Shackleton c Close b Clapp	0	— st Taylor b Breakwell	30
†A. J. Brassington not out	4	— not out	15
J. Davey b Botham	1	— b Botham	0
B 4, l-b 2, w 5, n-b 1	12	B 8, l-b 7, n-b 1	16

1/3 2/9 3/9 4/29   79   1/11 2/126 3/209   372
5/52 6/52 7/61 8/68 9/74   4/236 5/319 6/325 7/325
                         8/327 9/371

Bonus points—Somerset 4.

Bowling: *First Innings*—Clapp 13—6—18—3; Botham 16.1—6—25—6;
Jennings 8—1—24—1; Close 1—1—0—0; Kitchen 1—1—0—0. *Second Innings*—
Botham 37.1—6—125—5; Jennings 25—6—71—2; Close 27—9—90—2; Kitchen
3—0—21—0; Rose 4—0—9—0; Breakwell 24—12—40—1.

Note: Brassington kept wicket in the first innings, Stovold in the second.

Umpires: H. Horton and A. E. Fagg.

THE AUSTRALIANS

18, 19, 20 May 1977 at Bath

It was a brave committee decision to play the tourist match away from County headquarters, but the result justified the thinking and a wonderful three days were spent in the 'Georgian city'. They enjoyed superb weather, more reminiscent of Sydney than Somerset, plus three centurians, highly successful bowling by Burgess, Botham and Garner for Somerset and a great many no-balls from Jeff Thomson!

It was Somerset's 22nd attempt to beat the Aussies and with a magnificent century from their 'old boy', Greg Chappell – he was 99* at lunch – having cleared the boundary 3 times and reached it 14 times in his classical style all after Joel Garner had taken a wicket in his first over, their prospects were not looking too good.

Accurate bowling plus very good fielding saw Somerset fight back and the next 8 wickets yielded only 55 runs. The Australian total of 232 was at least 100 below expectations.

Somerset's openers, Rose and Denning, quickly saw the score into the 80s with Denning scoring a fine 39 – although he was helped by 15 no-balls from Thomson. Three important wickets fell with Richards (18), Close (0) and Breakwell (23) reducing them to 141 for 4. Brian Rose continued his patient innings, scoring an invaluable century, and Ian Botham scattered the crowd with 3 enormous sixes, making it possible to declare at 340 for 5.

Australia got off to another poor start and were soon 18 for 2, but David Hookes played one of his better innings, scoring 85* in 90 minutes before close of play on the second day. He went on to record 108 before Burgess came to Somerset's rescue by clean bowling him – his innings included 4 sixes and 15 fours – and the tourists were finally dismissed for 289.

Requiring 182 runs in 225 minutes was the Somerset target. Again, Rose and Denning made a good start with 50 at roughly a run per minute. Richards increased the tempo with a quick 53 before Botham arrived to score a typical 39* and at last Somerset had beaten the Australians. It was certainly party time in Bath.

Somerset v. Australia, Bath, 1977.

Australians

R. B. McCosker c Botham b Garner	2	– run out	2
C. S. Serjeant st Taylor b Burgess	13	– c Garner b Botham	50
*G. S. Chappell b Garner	113	– c Garner b Botham	39
G. J. Cosier b Garner	44	– c Taylor b Botham	2
K. D. Walters c Denning b Burgess	23	– b Botham	25
D. W. Hookes b Botham	3	– b Burgess	108
†R. W. Marsh b Garner	3	– b Garner	0
K. J. O'Keeffe c Denning b Burgess	11	– c Denning b Moseley	20
J. R. Thomson b Burgess	0	– c Botham b Garner	0
M. F. Malone b Burgess	2	– c Richards b Breakwell	17
G. Dymock not out	0	– not out	6
B 10, w 2, n-b 6	18	B 4, l-b 10, w 1, n-b 5	20

1/2 2/57 3/177 4/197 5/200   **232**
6/204 7/223 8/223 9/231

1/16 2/18 3/141   **289**
4/172 5/183 6/214 7/251
8/252 9/271

Bowling: *First Innings*—Garner 20–8–66–4; Moseley 16–5–52–0; Burgess 9.3–2–25–5; Botham 15–2–48–1; Breakwell 7–0–23–0. *Second Innings*—Garner 23–6–71–2; Moseley 17–6–55–1; Botham 22–6–98–4; Burgess 9–3–41–1; Breakwell 0.3–0–4–1.

Somerset

B. C. Rose not out	110	– c Marsh b Thomson	27
P. W. Denning c Marsh b Dymock	39	– b Chappell	34
I. V. A. Richards c Hookes b Malone	18	– c Cosier b O'Keeffe	53
*D. B. Close c McCosker b Malone	0		
D. Breakwell c Chappell b O'Keeffe	23		
I. T. Botham c McCosker b O'Keeffe	59	– not out	39
P. A. Slocombe not out	55	– not out	8
B 4, l-b 6, n-b 26	36	B 4, l-b 3, w 3, n-b 11	21

1/81 2/116 3/117   (5 wkts., dec.) **340**
4/146 5/228

1/50 2/129   (3 wkts.) **182**
3/129

G. I. Burgess, †D. J. S. Taylor, J. Garner and H. R. Moseley did not bat.

Bowling: *First Innings*—Thomson 16–2–60–0; Dymock 17–7–48–1; Malone 22–4–70–2; O'Keeffe 35–15–114–2; Chappell 2–0–11–0; Walters 2–1–1–0. *Second Innings*—Thomson 12–1–57–1; Malone 9–2–18–0; Chappell 8–4–29–1; Dymock 5–0–25–0; O'Keeffe 5.1–0–32–1.

Umpires H. D. Bird and T. W. Spencer

GLOUCESTERSHIRE

23, 25, 26 August 1980 at Bristol

In the return game of the 1980 season there were plenty of runs to satisfy the crowd but this time the excitement continued until the very last ball of the match. Gloucestershire batted first and though many of their batsmen never looked comfortable, they somehow reached 309. Dredge was by far the best of the Somerset bowlers, troubling all the batsmen, and his final figures of 5 for 95 hardly did him justice. Mike Procter and Graveney reached their fifties but the big wicket, that of Zaheer Abbas, had already fallen to a catch by Popplewell off Dredge.

When it was Somerset's turn to bat, Olive was out with the score of only 4, but then Viv Richards took over. Lloyd was out when 61 runs had been scored with Roebuck, and Richards plundered 3 sixes and 26 fours in a third-wicket partnership of 239 from only 51 overs. Richards reached a well deserved century, but the final total of 426 only gave Somerset a lead of 117.

Gloucestershire again lost an early wicket but Andy Stovold and Sadiq added 138. When Zaheer was unable to bat due to injury, it was left to Mike Procter to push the score along. He responded well by scoring a rapid 86 before being beautifully stumped by Gard from the bowling of Marks, who then proceeded to wrap up the tail, ending with 5 for 77 from 30 overs. This meant that Somerset had to score 201 to win.

A good start by Olive and Lloyd saw 70 on the board, but Somerset were handicapped by the absence of Richards through illness, and a rearranged batting order saw Vic Marks at number three. His brisk 32, before being stumped by Brassington, helped the score along but neither Denning nor Botham were successful and a far from fit Richards appeared, but was out without scoring.

With Roebuck and Dredge batting and the scores level, Roebuck needed a single from the last ball of the match for victory. After an appeal for lbw had been turned down, he attempted to run although the ball was in the wicketkeeper's gloves and the bails were off. Apparently, the umpire had called 'over' when he dismissed the lbw appeal and with the scores level, the Laws of Cricket had to be checked to ensure that the correct number of points were allocated to each side. With the Laws in force at the time, Somerset qualified for 6 extra points, being the side that had batted second!

Colin Dredge.

Mike Procter.

Schweppes County Championship: GLOUCESTERSHIRE v SOMERSET

at Bristol on 23rd, 25th, 26th August, 1980   Match tied

GLOUCESTERSHIRE

	First innings			Second innings	
A.W. Stovold	b Popplewell	37		c & b Lloyds	80
B.C. Broad	run out	0		c Popplewell b Gore	3
Sadiq	b Dredge	43		c Popplewell b Lloyds	92
Zaheer	c Popplewell b Dredge	5		Absent hurt	
*M.J. Procter	c Botham b Dredge	57		st Gard b Marks	84
M.D. Partridge	c Olive b Botham	48		c Olive b Marks	15
D.A. Graveney	c Richards b Dredge	55		c Botham b Marks	10
A.H. Wilkins	c Botham b Popplewell	32		b Marks	15
†A.J. Brassington	b Popplewell	12		b Marks	0
B.M. Brain	c Gard b Dredge	4		b Lloyds	1
J.H. Childs	not out	1		not out	0
Extras		15		Extras	17
TOTAL		309		Total	317

Fall of wickets: 1·6 2·69 3·74 4·112 5·161 6·224 7·274 8·290 9·299
1·14 2·152 3·272 4·276 5·300 6·313 7·316 8·317 9·317

Bowling:	O	M	R	W		O	M	R	W
Gore	12	3	34	0		13	2	48	1
Dredge	32	6	95	5		10	0	47	0
Popplewell	23·5	5	54	3		8	1	51	0
Richards	6	0	24	0					
Botham	14	5	55	1					
Marks	9	2	32	0		30	11	75	0
Lloyds						29·2	11	77	3

SOMERSET

	First innings			Second innings	
M. Olive	c Brassington b Brain	1		c Sadiq b Childs	21
J. Lloyds	c Brassington b Brain	33		c Partridge b Graveney	64
I.V.A. Richards	c Brain b Childs	170		c sub b Graveney	0
P.M. Roebuck	st Brassington b Childs	101		not out	37
P.W. Denning	c Procter b Wilkins	4		run out	1
*I.T. Botham	c Childs b Wilkins	18		c sub b Graveney	13
V.J. Marks	c Brassington b Childs	29		st Brassington b Graveney	32
N. Popplewell	st Brassington b Childs	19		b Brain	25
†T. Gard	b Procter	22			
C.H. Dredge	not out	13		not out	1
H. Gore	b Procter	4			
Extras		12		Extras	6
TOTAL		426		TOTAL (for 7 wkts)	200

Fall of wickets 1·4 2·61 3·300 4·311 5·333 6·342 7·371 8·390 9·420
1·70 2·96 3·104 4·119 5·140 6·140 7·197

Bowling:	O	M	R	W		O	M	R	W
Brain	20	1	91	2		8	2	32	1
Wilkins	24	5	94	2		4	0	24	0
Procter	2·5	0	13	2		2	0	12	0
Partridge	6	0	43	0					
Graveney	23	2	103	0		9	0	53	4
Childs	25	6	70	4		15	0	73	1

* Captain   † Wicketkeeper

115

GLOUCESTERSHIRE

13, 15, 16 June 1981 at Bath

Once again, Zaheer Abbas proved what a fine batsman he was and he seemed to save his best for matches against Somerset and this was no exception. He dominated the game throughout the three days, but even his superlative batting could not force a Gloucestershire victory. Somerset were indebted to two injured players, Rose and Roebuck, for valiantly saving the game when all seemed lost.

Batting first, Gloucestershire lost two quick wickets to Botham, but that was the end of Somerset's first-innings success. Enter Zaheer and it became an entirely different game, although he was dropped when he had scored 45. With Stovold he put on 188, of which Stovold scored 40, and then he shared a partnership of 122 with Hignell – his score was 215* when the declaration came at 361 for 4.

Somerset got off to a dreadful start, losing 5 wickets for 51 including Richards for 2, but Botham and Marks held firm and then Garner played an astonishing innings, hitting 4 sixes and 12 fours in scoring 90 – his highest score for Somerset. A total of 316 was far better than had been expected.

Once again it was nearly all Zaheer when Gloucestershire batted again. His final score of 150* included 1 six and 22 fours scored out of 216 and again Gloucestershire were able to declare at 303 for 4.

Leaving Somerset a target of 349 in 200 minutes was far from generous, especially as both Ross and Roebuck had sustained injuries whilst fielding and were unlikely to bat.

The visitors were also without a leading player as Brain was unable to bowl and a rearranged batting order never looked like saving the game when 6 wickets fell for 79. Breakwell followed his 58 in the first innings with a gallant 53 and stern defence by Moseley and Garner gave Somerset some hope. With 90 minutes left, Brian Rose entered at number ten and with an attacking field decided to play his shots, finding the boundary on numerous occasions and when the 9th wicket fell the second 'cripple' found his way to the wicket, but there still remained 45 minutes of playing time.

All attempts by the Gloucestershire bowlers were withstood and at close of play Rose had reached 85*, including 19 boundaries, and Roebuck 13*. Against all the odds, Somerset had saved the game.

Zaheer Abbas.

Schweppes County Championship: SOMERSET v GLOUCESTERSHIRE   Gloucs won toss

At Bath on June 13th, 15th, 16th 1981   Match Drawn

GLOUCESTERSHIRE

	First innings		Second Innings	
C.B. Broad	lbw b Botham	11	c & b Lloyds	37
Sadiq Mohammad	lbw b Botham	23	c Denning b Marks	33
§A.W. Stovold	b Moseley	40	run out	21
Zaheer Abbas	not out	215	not out	150
A.J. Hignall	run out	55	not out	40
P. Bainbridge	not out	3	b Moseley	12
S.J. Windybank				
D.A. Graveney				
A.H. Wilkens				
*B.M. Brain				
J.H. Childs				
Extras		14	Extras	10
TOTAL (for 4 wkts dec)		361	TOTAL (for 4 wkts dec)	303

Fall of wickets: 1-30 2-36 3-224 4-346
1-64 2-82 3-87 4-182

Bowling:	O	M	R	W	O	M	R	W
Garner	26	4	81	0	10	3	20	0
Botham	25	7	99	2	9	1	45	0
Richards	7	2	26	0	13	1	53	0
Moseley	15	2	56	1	10	2	21	1
Breakwell	14	4	56	0				
Marks	13	2	40	0	28	4	74	1
Lloyds	3	0	16	0	14	3	64	1
Denning					1	0	16	0

SOMERSET

	First innings		Second Innings	
*B.C. Rose	c Stovold b Wilkens	21	not out	85
J.W. Lloyds	c Windaybank b Bainbridge	6	c Stovold b Bainbridge	2
I.V.A. Richards	b Bainbridge	2	c Graveney b Wilkens	37
P.W. Denning	c Hignell b Wilkens	8	lbw b Wilkens	12
I.T. Botham	c Stovold b Bainbridge	41	b Bainbridge	1
V.J. Marks	c Sadiq b Brain	49	c Childs b Bainbridge	9
§D.J.S. Taylor	c Bainbridge b Brain	18	b Bainbridge	4
D. Breakwell	c Childs b Graveney	58	lbw b Wilkens	53
H.R. Moseley	not out	2	c Graveney b Childs	10
J. Garner	b Wilkens	90	c Sadiq b Bainbridge	16
P.M. Roebuck	absent hurt		not out	13
Extras		21	Extras	3
TOTAL		316	TOTAL (for 9 wkts)	245

Fall of wickets: 1-27 2-29 3-42 4-51 5-106 6-163 7-164 8-286 9-316
1-14 2-20 3-52 4-52 5-67 6-79 7-125 8-137 9-200

Bowling:	O	M	R	W	O	M	R	W
Brain	14	2	60	2				
Wilkens	24	9	50	3	21	3	139	3
Childs	19	3	83	0	11	6	15	1
Bainbridge	18	3	58	3	20	7	68	5
Broad	5	1	18	0	3	0	15	0
Graveney	6	1	26	1	3	1	5	0

Umpires: B. Leadbeater & P.B. Wight

*Captain   §Wicketkeeper

WARWICKSHIRE

1, 3, 5 June 1985 at Taunton

There was no hesitation when Vic Marks won the toss – Somerset would bat. Was it to be regretted when Ball had to retire hurt having scored only 8 and Felton failing to score? Enter Viv Richards and the smiles were soon back on the supporters' faces for they were to be treated to one of the greatest examples of batsmanship seen for many years.

He reached 100 from only 105 balls and incredibly his tempo actually increased with his second 100 taking only 76 balls. Could this 'murder' continue? Yes it could and his next 100 was to be faster still, needing only 63 balls. Batting under 5 hours, facing 258 deliveries, he hit 8 sixes and 42 fours in a display that will never be forgotten by those present.

Declaring at 566 for 9, the only hope of victory was to get some quick wickets and be in a position to enforce the follow-on. Sadly neither occurred and Warwickshire's batting was sound, with P.A. Smith scoring 93 and Ferreira an undefeated 101 out of a total of 442 for 9 declared.

'Joke' bowling enabled Somerset to score a rapid 226 for 5 before declaring without any help from Richards who did not bat, but Vic Marks followed up his first innings 65 with 66* leaving Warwickshire 351 to get for victory.

It was all to no avail as Warwickshire showed no interest in chasing this total though over the three and a half hours of play remained and on a typical Taunton wicket this could well have been within their reach.

A tame draw resulted but this was still an unforgettable game due to one of the great 'knocks' of the 1980s.

Vic Marks.

SOMERSET v WARWICKSHIRE

at Taunton on 1st, 3rd and 4th June, 1985

Somerset won toss

Match Drawn

SOMERSET

	1st Innings		2nd Innings	
N.F.M. Popplewell	c Tedstone b Hoffman	55	c Hoffman b Small	27
P.A. Bail	retired hurt	8	c Kallicharran b Small	0
N. Felton	c Kallicharran b Small	0	c Small b Lloyd	45
I.V.A. Richards	b Ferreira	322		
R.L. Ollis	c Hoffman b Ferreira	55	lbw b Wall	0
*V.J. Marks	st Tedstone b Gifford	65	not out	66
§T. Gard			run out	47
M.S. Turner	not out	17	not out	24
M.R. Davis	not out	25		
J. Garner				
S.C. Booth				
	B 1, Lb 9, W 1, Nb 8	19	Lb 13, Nb 4	17
	TOTAL (for 5 wkts dec)	566	TOTAL (for 5 wkts dec)	226

1st inns: 1-28 2-150 3-324 4-507 5-533
2nd inns: 1-1 2-62 3-103 4-105 5-175

Warwicks Bowling	O	M	R	W	O	M	R	W
Small	16	3	70	1	8	0	31	2
Wall	18	3	72	0	5	2	7	1
Smith	11	0	73	0	9	1	43	0
Ferreira	23	0	121	2				
Hoffman	14	0	85	1	2	0	12	0
Gifford	18	1	135	1				
Lloyd					16	0	64	1
Kallicharran					11.4	0	56	2

WARWICKS

	1st Innings		2nd Innings	
T.A. Lloyd	lbw b Richards	61	c Gard b Garner	7
R.I.H.B. Dyer	lbw b Turner	33	not out	63
A.I. Kallicharran	c Garner b Davis	36	c Gard b Marks	89
D.L. Amiss	c Davis b Marks	81	not out	14
§G.A. Tedstone	b Turner	22		
P.A. Smith	c Turner b Marks	93		
A.M. Ferreira	not out	101		
G.C. Small	c Davis b Turner	3		
S. Wall	lbw b Turner	1		
*N. Gifford	not out	0		
D.S. Hoffman	run out	0		
	B 1, Lb 6, W 1, Nb 3	11	Lb 5, W 1, Nb 2	8
	TOTAL (for 9 wkts dec)	442	TOTAL (for 2 wkts)	181

1st inns: 1-84 2-108 3-151 4-312 5-312 6-399 7-419 8-431 9-431
2nd inns: 1-18 2-158

Somerset Bowling	O	M	R	W	O	M	R	W
Garner	20	3	59	0	6	2	16	1
Davis	23.4	1	115	1	9	2	19	0
Turner	22.4	2	74	4	1	0	9	0
Richards	12	4	31	1				
Marks	25	3	97	2	16	1	56	1
Booth	13	3	59	0	21	4	72	0
Bail					2	0	4	0

Umpires: A.A. Jones & P.B. Wight

*Captain §Wicketkeeper

WORCESTERSHIRE

5, 6, 7, 9 May 1988 at Taunton

There was a perfect Taunton batting wicket and on losing the toss, Somerset had their hopes raised when they captured the first 5 wickets for only 132 runs including the wicket of their former captain, Ian Botham, for only 7.

Watching this decline from the other end was a certain G.A. Hick, who suddenly took over. While he had his moments of good fortune, he was to become only the seventh batsman in the history of the game to score over 400 in a single innings.

He had entered the 'battlefield' with the score on 78 for 1 roughly 30 minutes before lunch, yet he was able to enjoy one of the best lunches on the circuit with 31* to his credit – and much better was to follow. After the fall of 4 quick wickets he found the perfect partner in wicket-keeper, Steve Rhodes, and by close of play Worcestershire were 312 for 5 with Hick 179*.

The second day saw him progress in perfect style without giving a chance. His first 100 had taken 126 balls, his second 151 balls and his third 134 balls in a total time of just over 8 hours. With a declaration in the offering he then proceeded to score his fourth 100 in only 71 minutes – this included 8 sixes and 6 fours, moving the score from 399 to 405 from the second-last ball before tea.

The declaration came when Hick was within 20 runs of the all-time record score by a batsman in England that had been held by A.C. MacLaren since 1895 (again scored at Taunton). Was the declaration made in the interests of the game or were the captain and batsman unaware of this record?

The final result was a crushing victory for Worcestershire with Somerset forced to follow on, having been dismissed for a mediocre 222, Dilley and Radford each taking 4 wickets with no Somerset batsman reaching 50. It was even worse in the second innings, with the home side failing to reach 200 and defeat by an innings and 214 runs was all they deserved.

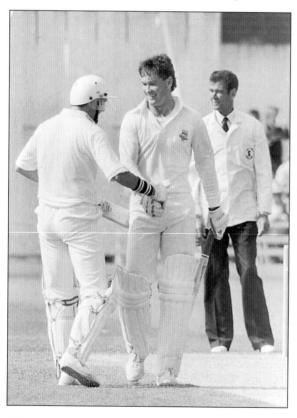

Graeme Hick being congratulated after scoring 400.

SOMERSET v. WORCESTERSHIRE (4 Day Match)

Britannic Assurance Championship
At Taunton 5th, 6th, 7th, 9th May 1988
Umpires: R. Julian/R. Palmer
Scorers: D.A. Oldam/J.W. Sewter

Worcester won Toss
Worcester won by innings and 214
Somerset 4pts, Worcester 23pts
Somerset MoM: M.D. Crowe

WORCESTER

	1st Innings		2nd Innings	
T.S. Curtis	b Rose	27		
G.J. Lord	c Mallender b Dredge	49		
G.A. Hick	not out	405		
D.B. D'Oliveira	c Roebuck b Rose	0		
*P.A. Neale	c Marks b Mallender	0		
I.T. Botham	b Rose	7		
§S.J. Rhodes	c Felton b Dredge	56		
P.J. Newport	b Marks	27		
R.K. Illingworth	not out	31		
N.V. Radford				
G.R. Dilley				
	B6, Lb16, Nb4	26		
	TOTAL (for 7 wkts dec)	628		

1st inns: 1-78 2-112 3-112 4-119 5-132 6-397 7-451
Bonus points: Somerset 2; Worcester 3 (score at 100 overs: 287-5)

Somerset Bowling	O	M	R	W	O	M	R	W
Jones	32	4	97	0				
Mallender	32	9	86	1				
Marks	50	6	141	1				
Rose	31	8	101	3				
Dredge	34.5	8	133	2				
Roebuck	10	0	48	0				

SOMERSET

	1st Innings		2nd Innings	
N.A. Felton	c Radford b Hick	24	c Rhodes b Newport	36
*P.M. Roebuck	lbw b Radford	0	lbw b Radford	17
J.J.E. Hardy	c Rhodes b Radford	39	b Newport	0
M.D. Crowe	c Rhodes b Newport	28	c Lord b Radford	53
R.J. Harden	lbw b Hick	2	lbw b Newport	3
V.J. Marks	c Botham b Newport	42	c Hick b Newport	7
§N.D. Burns	c Botham b Radford	32	c Illingworth b Hick	11
G.D. Rose	c Curtis b Newport	12	c Rhodes b Newport	30
N.A. Mallender	c Rhodes b Newport	3	lbw b Radford	1
C.H. Dredge	b Radford	16	c Curtis b Newport	17
A.N. Jones	not out	8	not out	3
	Lb6, Nb10	16	B2, Lb1, Nb11	14
	TOTAL (All out)	222	TOTAL (All out)	192

1st inns: 1-1 2-70 3-70 4-75 5-147 6-152 7-166 8-173 9-203
2nd inns: 1-49 2-59 3-62 4-74 5-90 6-111 7-154 8-167 9-185
Bonus points: Somerset 2; Worcester 4

Worcester Bowling	O	M	R	W	O	M	R	W
Dilley	12	0	40	0	14	2	40	0
Radford	23.5	1	77	4	17	6	39	3
Newport	17	4	59	4	15.3	3	50	6
Hick	8	3	18	2	11	4	15	1
Illingworth	1	0	4	0	11	4	20	0
Botham	9	3	18	0	6	2	25	0

*Captain   §Wicketkeeper

LANCASHIRE

2, 3, 4 July 1991 at Taunton

Somerset's centenary year had not started well, with 8 drawn Championship games and a defeat by Glamorgan out of their first matches. It was also an experimental season with some three-day and some four-day Championship matches making up the Championship table.

Lancashire arrived at Taunton with 4 victories to their credit against only one defeat, and were obviously favourites to win in what was to be a three-day game. Winning the toss, they had no hesitation in electing to bat and a superb 109 by Neil Fairbrother fully justified this decision. With runs from Wasim Akram, they were able to declare with 326 runs on the board for the loss of 8 wickets. There was still time for Somerset to score 39 before stumps were drawn at the end of the first day.

1991 was to be Jimmy Cook's final year and runs continued to pour from his bat. His 131 contained 17 boundaries, but he once again lacked real support. Somerset's scoring rate was poor and when the total had reached 268 for 3, there was a suprise declaration by Chris Tavare. Two quick wickets fell and by the end of the second day Lancashire had reached 67 for the loss of 2 wickets. Once again Neil Fairbrother proved his class as a batsman and had scored his second century, 102*, when Lancashire felt able to declare, leaving Somerset to score 294 in just over three hours.

Cook and Roebuck were unable to score at the required rate, 100 runs taking 30 overs, but Chris Tavare's arrival helped the score along – he scored a quick-fire 50 from only 57 balls before being tragically run out. 20 overs to go and still 150 runs required for victory – surely an impossible feat? For Somerset on their day, anything was possible! Ken MacLeay, who was having a disappointing season with the ball, struck a six on four occasions and took only 27 balls in scoring 36 runs and with Neil Burns keeping the scoreboard ticking over, there were still 46 runs required from the last 5 overs.

Andy Hayhurst, batting at number eight, gave Dutchman Roland LeFebvre support and the target was reached with only two balls left. It was an exciting first victory of the season, but they had to wait until the middle of September before earning a second and their centenary ended with them bottom of the Championship table.

Neil Fairbrother.

SOMERSET v. LANCASHIRE

Britannic Assurance Championship
At Taunton July 2, 3, 4th 1991
Umpires: D. J. Constant/B. Dudleston
Scorers: D. A. Oldam/W. Davies

Lancashire won Toss
Somerset won by 4 wickets
Somerset 22pts, Lancashire 5pts

LANCASHIRE	1st Innings		2nd Innings	
G. D. Mendis	c & b Trump	31	b Lefebvre	1
G. Fowler	c & b MacLeay	14	lbw b Mallender	0
N. J. Speak	c Harden b MacLeay	56	c Graveney b Lefebvre	49
N. H. Fairbrother	c MacLeay b Roebuck	109	not out	102
S. P. Titchard	c Burns b Lefebvre	53	b Lefevre	0
M. Watkinson	c Harden b Trump	13	c Graveney b Harden	30
Wasim Akram	b Trump	39	lbw b Harden	2
¶W. G. Hegg	not out	0	(6) c Burns b MacLeay	17
G. Yates	lbw b Lefebvre	0	not out	27
*D. P. Hughes				
P. J. Martin				
	B4, LB1, W2, NB4	11	B4, LB1, NB2	7
	TOTAL (8 wkts dec)	326	TOTAL (7 wkts dec)	237

1st inns: 1-24, 2-66, 3-177, 4-233, 5-276, 6-326, 7-326, 8-326
2nd inns: 1-1, 2-2, 3-76, 4-82, 5-129, 6-180, 7-182
Bonus Points: Lancashire 4, Somerset 3

Somerset Bowling	O	M	R	W		O	M	R	W
Mallender	15	3	42	0		3	0	6	1
Lefebvre	13.2	3	48	2		16	1	54	3
MacLeay	18	5	42	2		17	5	39	1
Hayhurst	8	0	39	0		2	2	0	0
Trump	15	2	47	3		28	8	45	0
Graveney	16	4	61	0					
Roebuck	13	1	42	1		11	3	16	0
Harden						13	0	70	2

SOMERSET	1st Innings		2nd Innings	
S. J. Cook	c Speak b Watkinson	131	st Hegg b Hughes	61
P. M. Roebuck	c Hegg b Hughes	46	c Titchard b Yates	52
A. N. Hayhurst	c Titchard b Martin	29	(8) not out	22
*C. J. Tavare			run out	50
R. J. Harden	not out	29	c Titchard b Yates	12
¶N. D. Burns	not out	27	c Fairbrother b Watkinson	25
K. H. MacLeay			c & b Yates	36
R. P. Lefebvre			not out	23
N. A. Mallender				
H. R. J. Trump				
D. A. Graveney				
	LB4, W1, NB1	6	B6, LB5, W1, NB1	13
	TOTAL (3 wkts dec)	268	TOTAL (6 wkts)	294

1st inns: 1-86, 2-206, 3-216
2nd inns: 1-104, 2-124, 3-144, 4-197, 5-238, 6-248
Bonus Points: Somerset 3, Lancashire 3

Lancashire Bowling	O	M	R	W		O	M	R	W
Wasim Akram	3	1	7	0		7	2	25	0
Martin	13	0	42	1					
Watkinson	21	3	70	1		11	0	85	1
Yates	26	8	59	0		23.4	3	83	3
Hughes	32	3	86	1		19	4	90	1

*Captain   ¶Wicketkeeper

WARWICKSHIRE
17, 18, 19, 20 September 1991 at Taunton

Firmly entrenched at the bottom of the championship table, Somerset were hoping to end the season with a victory – but it was not to be. In beautiful September weather on a typical Taunton wicket and Jimmy Cook making his farewell appearance there was a good crowd to watch what turned out to be one of the best games of the season. Warwickshire won the toss and had no hesitation in batting first and by close of play they had reached 316 for 7, with half-centuries from captain, Andy Lloyd, Ratcliffe and Ostler. Somerset were reasonably happy with their day's work and had it not been for a fine 62 from Booth, Warwickshire would not have attained a final total of 376. Neil Mallender bowled extremely well in taking 6 for 68 and when Somerset batted no one was surprised when Jimmy Cook registered his 11th century of the season, breaking records that had stood for years. Batting failures, however, meant that by close of play on the second day Somerset were all out for 289 – a deficit of 87.

Sound all-round batting by the visitors, with Ratcliffe scoring a brisk 84, left Somerset with the task of scoring 409 runs from a minimum of 122 overs and they had reached 60 for the loss of one wicket by the close of play on the third day.

Could they manage 349 runs on the final in fine weather on a still good batting track? Jimmy Cook and Richard Harden got them off to a good start but disaster occurred when the slow left-arm bowling accounted for Jimmy Cook and worse was to follow when he also deceived Chris Tavare. All was not lost whilst Graham Rose and Ken MacLeay remained – they added 55 at better than a run a ball, and victory became a possibility, if not quite a probability. At 387 for 8 there were four possible results but the recall of Booth proved too much for Somerset and they were ultimately defeated by the small margin of 5 runs.

In the evening, a farewell dinner for Jimmy Cook was held in the Colin Atkinson pavilion that was overcrowded with members wishing to thank him for his three incredible years as Somerset's overseas player.

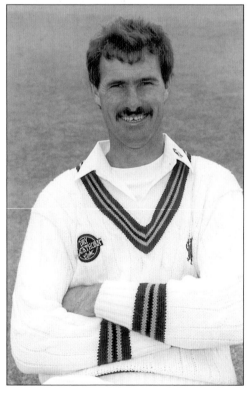

Jimmy Cook.

SOMERSET v. WARWICKSHIRE

Britannic Assurance Championship
At Taunton September 17, 18, 19, 20th 1991
Umpires: D. R. Shepherd/R. C. Tolchard
Scorers: D. A. Oldam/S. P. Austin

Warwickshire won Toss
Warwickshire won by 5 runs
Somerset 6pts, Warwickshire 23pts

WARWICKSHIRE

	1st Innings		2nd Innings	
A. J. Moles	c Bartlett b Graveney	26	c Trump b Rose	1
J. D. Ratcliffe	c MacLeay b Mallender	61	c Rose b Trump	84
*T. A. Lloyd	c Trump b Graveney	69	c Cook b Graveney	18
D. P. Ostler	c Tavare b Trump	79	b Rose	58
D. A. Reeve	lbw b Mallender	11	c Lefebvre b Rose	57
Asif Din	b Mallender	11	b Mallender	34
N. M. K. Smith	lbw b Mallender	2	b Mallender	1
¶K. J. Piper	c Burns b Mallender	35	b Rose	30
P. A. Booth	c Rose b Trump	62	c Cook b Graveney	0
T. A. Munton	not out	6	not out	12
A. A. Donald	b Mallender	4	not out	8
	LB4, NB6	10	B2, LB14, W1, NB1	18
	TOTAL (all out)	376	TOTAL (9 wkts dec)	321

1st inns: 1-74, 2-95, 3-225, 4-249, 5-255, 6-257, 7-270, 8-362, 9-365
2nd inns: 1-11, 2-46, 3-161, 4-175, 5-241, 6-243, 7-278, 8-285, 9-309
Bonus Points: Warwickshire 3, Somerset 3

Somerset Bowling	O	M	R	W		O	M	R	W
Mallender	28.2	7	68	6		16	4	55	2
Rose	18	2	70	0		20	3	77	4
Trump	32	10	95	2		19	2	69	1
Graveney	26	6	73	2		24	3	79	2
Lefebvre	12	4	27	0		8	0	25	0
MacLeay	7	0	39	0					

SOMERSET

	1st Innings		2nd Innings	
S. J. Cook	c Piper b Booth	127	c Ratcliffe b Booth	40
¶N. D. Burns	b Donald	5	b Donald	0
R. J. Harden	b Booth	5	c Reeve b Smith	68
*C. J. Tavare	lbw b Munton	0	b Booth	85
R. J. Bartlett	lbw b Reeve	38	c Ostler b Reeve	35
K. H. MacLeay	c Ostler b Donald	63	c Piper b Reeve	47
G. D. Rose	c Ostler b Donald	10	c Piper b Munton	55
R. P. Lefebvre	b Donald	6	c Ratcliffe b Smith	15
N. A. Mallender	b Donald	6	not out	13
H. R. J. Trump	b Donald	8	b Booth	4
D. A. Graveney	not out	2	b Booth	8
	B4, LB8, NB7	19	B14, LB13, NB6	33
	TOTAL (all out)	289	TOTAL (all out)	403

1st inns: 1-18, 2-46, 3-51, 4-117, 5-243, 6-251, 7-257, 8-275, 9-280
2nd inns: 1-3, 2-89, 3-132, 4-224, 5-290, 6-320, 7-362, 8-382, 9-387
Bonus Points: Somerset 3, Warwickshire 4

Warwickshire Bowling	O	M	R	W		O	M	R	W
Donald	20.2	2	84	6		23	4	95	1
Munton	20	5	52	1		18	5	57	1
Booth	27	6	76	2		43.1	10	103	4
Smith	11	2	38	0		28	6	79	2
Reeve	6	1	27	1		13	1	36	2
Din						1	0	6	0

*Captain   ¶Wicketkeeper

LANCASHIRE

13, 14 May 1993 at Taunton

Somerset had an encouraging start to the 1993 season, with an early victory over Hampshire and a credible performance against the touring Australians, followed by an incredible victory over a strong Lancashire at Taunton.

Somerset gave a debut to the young and very promising Marcus Trescothick and on winning the toss he found himself opening the batting with Mark Lathwell. It was hoped that this young pair would become the recognised Somerset openers for years to come and perhaps even open for England. Mark did go on to play for England within a year, but Marcus had to wait until 2000 before he finally reached the Test match stage. Injuries and loss of form have so far prevented this exciting partnership from achieving its expected potential.

A quiet start to the game saw Somerset lose their first 3 wickets for only 12 runs, but Mushtaq Ahmed, making his Championship debut, and Andy Caddick saw them through to 195 with De Freitas taking 7 wickets for 76 runs. Lancashire then found runs hard to come by and with the wickets shared between Caddick, Rose and Mushtaq the last 4 wickets fell for only 18 runs and Somerset were somewhat fortunate to be trailing by only 27.

De Freitas again proved to be Lancashire's best bowler, and Somerset's final total of 114 was due to some highly unorthodox batting by Van Troost. He scored 35 from only 28 balls in raising the score from 72 for 9 to 114 all out, which left Lancashire with what was expected to be a simple task of scoring 88 runs to win.

Chris Tavare, Somerset's captain, opened the bowling with Caddick and Mushtaq. Within minutes, the apparently impossible task of removing the opposition for less than 88 became a real probability, as the first 6 wickets fell for only 16 runs, with Caddick, aided by some superb catching, taking 5 of them.

There was panic in the Lancashire dressing room, with captain Neil Fairbrother, who was already out, trying to encourage his remaining batsmen – but to no avail. Mike Watkinson scored a valuable 39, but it was to be Andy Caddick's day, taking the last 4 wickets and ending up with career best figures of 9 for 32.

This was a great victory against all the odds and the game was over by 5.30p.m. of the second day.

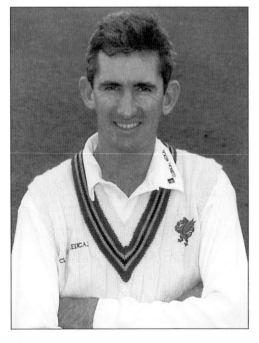

Andy Caddick.

SOMERSET v. LANCASHIRE

Britannic Assurance Championship
At Taunton 13, 14 May 1993
Umpires: R. Palmer/J. C. Balderstone
Scorers: D. A. Oldam/W. Davies

Somerset won Toss
Somerset won by 15 runs
Somerset 20pts, Lancashire 5pts

SOMERSET

	1st Innings		2nd Innings	
M. N. Lathwell	c Atherton b DeFreitas	71	c Hegg b Wasim Akram	5
M. E. Trescothick	lbw b DeFreitas	1	c Hegg b DeFreitas	3
R. J. Harden	c Hegg b DeFreitas	0	b DeFreitas	18
*C. J. Tavare	c sub b DeFreitas	3	c Atherton b DeFreitas	3
N. A. Folland	c Atherton b Martin	26	c Atherton b Wasim Akram	6
¶N. D. Burns	b DeFreitas	10	b Wasim Akram	3
G. D. Rose	b DeFreitas	8	lbw b Wasim Akram	13
A. R. Caddick	c Hegg b Wasim Akram	22	lbw b DeFreitas	9
Mustaq Ahmed	lbw b DeFreitas	24	lbw b DeFreitas	4
H. R. J. Trump	c Hegg b Wasim Akram	0	not out	3
A. P. Van Troost	not out	9	c DeFreitas b Martin	35
	B1, LB8, W2, NB10	21	LB2, NB10	12
	TOTAL (all out)	195	TOTAL (all out)	114

1st inns: 1-4, 2-4, 3-12, 4-91, 5-127, 6-140, 7-145, 8-181, 9-181
2nd inns: 1-9, 2-9, 3-16, 4-31, 5-41, 6-49, 7-66, 8-66, 9-72
Bonus Points: Lancashire 4

Lancashire Bowling	O	M	R	W	O	M	R	W
Wasim Akram	15	1	45	2	18	5	42	4
DeFreitas	17.3	4	76	7	17	2	55	5
Martin	11	1	35	1	1.2	0	15	1
Watkinson	4	1	13	0				
Barnett	8	3	17	0				

LANCASHIRE

	1st Innings		2nd Innings	
G. D. Mendis	b Mushtaq Ahmed	37	c Harden b Caddick	0
M. A. Atherton	lbw b Rose	21	c Tavare b Caddick	0
N. J. Speak	b Rose	58	lbw b Mushtaq Ahmed	1
G. D. Lloyd	c Burns b Caddick	16	lbw b Caddick	5
¶W. K. Hegg	c Tavare b Mushtaq Ahmed	5	c Harden b Caddick	0
Wasim Akram	c Folland b Mushtaq Ahmed	39	c & b Caddick	11
*N. H. Fairbrother	b Rose	0	c Burns b Caddick	5
M. Watkinson	c Burns b Caddick	21	b Caddick	39
P. A. J. DeFreitas	c Folland b Mushtaq Ahmed	6	c Folland b Caddick	0
P. J. Martin	not out	6	lbw b Caddick	5
A. A. Barnett	lbw b Caddick	0	not out	5
	LB10, W1, NB2	13	LB1	1
	TOTAL (all out)	222	TOTAL (all out)	72

1st inns: 1-50, 2-76, 3-117, 4-130, 5-153, 6-153, 7-204, 8-208, 9-220
2nd inns: 1-0, 2-1, 3-1, 4-1, 5-8, 6-16, 7-39, 8-39, 9-65
Bonus Points: Lancashire 1, Somerset 4

Somerset Bowling	O	M	R	W	O	M	R	W
Caddick	23.2	4	88	3	11.1	2	32	9
Van Troost	8	2	24	0				
Rose	13	2	60	3				
Mushtaq Ahmed	14	2	40	4	11	3	39	1

*Captain   ¶Wicketkeeper

Marcus Trescothick.